This book is a gift to

from the Next Steps Liaison
Project

POWER SOURCE
Taking Charge of Your Life

by Bethany Casarjian
and Robin Casarjian

LIONHEART PRESS

The Lionheart Foundation
PO Box 170115
Boston, MA 02117

Printed in the United States of America

ISBN: 978-0-9644933-4-6
Library of Congress Catalog Card Number: 2002095956

Book design by Cathy Bobak

6 7 8 9 10

First printing, 2003
(20,000 copies)

Second printing, 2004
(20,000 copies)

Third printing, 2006
(10,000 copies)

Fourth printing, 2007
(15,000 copies)

Fifth printing, 2013
(5,000 copies)

Sixth printing, 2018
(5,000 copies)

This project would not have been possible without the help of people who had the courage to tell the stories that are in this book. We want to thank the young men and women who contributed to this book. Many participated in the groups that were held while this book was being written. Their voices and wisdom are in every page.

A special thanks to. . .

ROCA (Chelsea, MA)

The Children's Village (Dobbs Ferry, NY)

Center for Community Alternatives (New York, NY)

Youthful Offender Program: Ohio Department of Correction and Rehabilitation

Contents

You and This Book

I started getting into trouble when I was 11 or 12, hanging out with the older crowd on the corner. I sold weed and coke and did things that would make me fit in with those guys. My mom was never around and my father was not present in my life. My family didn't show up for me or make me feel like I belong in this world.

I was angry and hurt because my parents weren't there. I thought I could run from the hurt of not feeling any love. To me it felt like they didn't care about me. So why should I care about myself? Behaving negatively and acting out my anger by harming others made me feel powerful. It made me feel like no one could ever hurt me again. I felt like I was in control of my anger, but I wasn't. I wanted someone to tell me to stop. But my actions fell on deaf ears. No one noticed so I started to get into street life deeper and deeper until it got a real good hold on me.

The more trouble I got into, the worse I felt. My anger grew and I got more mad at myself for doin' stupid shit over and over.

James, 18 years old

Who Is This Book For?

When we wrote this book, we wanted it to be for young men and women who struggle every day with hard choices, tough family situations, and big questions about their futures. It is filled with the voices of teenagers facing the same challenges that you might be dealing with right now—drugs, anger, violence, gangs, and questions about who you really are. And while this book doesn't have all the answers, it can definitely help you uncover *the power, strength, and wisdom that already exist inside of you.* The power might be hiding or out of sight. But make no mistake. . . it is there.

This book is for anyone who is tired of getting into trouble or making decisions that cause them to lose their freedom. It's for anyone who wants to have a better life, but isn't sure how to make that happen. This book will help you discover *who you really are and where you want to go*. By helping you figure out some of these things, the book can be a source of power. But this book is based on a simple truth: *Only you have the power to decide where you'll end up. You* are the real power source.

No matter what has happened in the past, no matter what you believe your future might be like, no matter what anyone has told you about the kind of life you will lead, your life is just beginning, even if you feel like it's over. In the back of your mind, you might believe that the story of your life has already been written. Think again.

How to Use This Book

There are many ways to use this book. And you don't have to read or write. Many people have a hard time reading. Maybe there is a group of people who can read it together. Be creative. There's no right or wrong way to get something from this book.

Sometimes the topics in the book can bring up feelings that make you feel uncomfortable, turn you off, or upset you. **Don't Let This Stop You**. If you start to feel overwhelmed, let someone know. This could be a trusted adult. There are always people who can help, even if it means calling a number provided at the back of this book. When you are ready, return to the book again.

Because it is a book, you can read it as fast or as slowly as you want. You can think about things at your own pace. And because you can read this book privately, you may find yourself able to be more honest with yourself than you can be when talking to other people.

Other Things to Know

We have worked with many kids who have gone to jail, prison, residential treatment centers, and foster care. We have talked to kids who have been hurt and who have hurt others. We think that this book has a lot of truth in it. And we believe that these truths can give you a great deal of power.

We try not to assume to know how you feel or what your life has been like. Nobody knows that but you.

We don't know where everyone is coming from. We all have different family backgrounds. Some are "traditional" and some are not. Throughout this book when we say "parent," we mean anyone who has been responsible for raising you. This can include biological parents, foster parents, grandparents, aunts, uncles, or anyone else who has cared for you.

Most of all, we believe that each one of you reading this book has a lot to give to the world. You are strong, powerful, loving, and wise. You might not be connected to those things within you at the moment, but they are there. They are waiting to come out. It is your decision whether you take these gifts out and share them or whether you bury them forever. Only you can make that decision. Only you have that power.

Chapter 1

Risk Taking: Life on the Edge

I'm only 18 and I been through shit that grown men haven't even seen. I've been locked up, I've been shot at—I done some crazy-ass shit. I'm lucky to still be alive, breathin' and eatin'.

Oonald, 18 years old

I remember the first time I was arrested. I was drivin' around in a stolen car with my girls. We was just chillin' and smokin' some weed. One of the girls decided to drive to New Hampshire and I didn't give a shit because I was just like, "whatever." But once we got onto the highway, we got lost and scared because we were high and didn't know what to do. Then a cop pulled us over and arrested us 'cause he found out that the car was stolen.

When they locked us up they took off my clothes to see if I had any drugs, and then they took our fingerprints and count our tattoos and I didn't like them touchin' me and doin' all that stuff to my body. It was no fun at all. And when my brother and father came to get me, I was cryin' and ashamed. They didn't even speak to me, they was so mad. While we was high and crusin' it seemed good, but I ain't never want to be locked up like that again.

Jennifer, 17 years old

High-Risk Behavior

Chances are that if you are reading this book, you have already been involved in some high-risk behaviors. Just so that we are all speaking the same language, let us lay out what we mean by high-risk behaviors.

Negative High-Risk Behaviors are activities that will probably mess you up at some point. Maybe the harm won't come the first time you try it, but over time, watch out. The danger could be *physical harm*, like hurting yourself with a weapon or drugs, getting sick from unprotected sex, getting hit by a car or getting into a fight and winding up in the hospital, getting killed or killing someone else. The harm could also be *suffering consequences* for your actions, like losing your freedom by going to jail, getting an arrest record, being suspended from school, or feeling like your life is going nowhere.

Other High-Risk Behaviors

There are other types of risky behavior that could possibly be dangerous, but they are meant for sport or recreation. They give you a *rush*, a *thrill or a high*, but they are not considered illegal, criminal, or antisocial (things that violate the rights of others). Think about skateboarding, motorcycle riding, skydiving, and rock climbing. These things are not what we are talking about when we say high-risk behavior.

You might be doing some pretty high-risk behaviors that seem totally ordinary and normal to you. Take a minute and look at this list. If you disagree about some of the things we put down, check it out with someone else. See what they think. Think about what the consequences of these activities might be. *Remember, it is the possible consequences that make these things high risk.*

High-Risk Activities

Stealing →

Drinking or Drugging →

Unprotected Sex →

Carrying a Weapon →

Driving with no License →

Ignoring Curfew →

Dealing Drugs →

Fighting →

Hitchhiking →

Driving While Drunk or High →

Messing Around with Someone → Else's Boyfriend/Girlfriend

Resisting Arrest →

Having Sex as Part of a → Gang Initiation

Gang Banging →

Consequences to You

What's in It for Me When I Take a Risk?

Why do people choose to live risky lives? Well, let's be honest. You take a risk because you *get something out of it*. High-risk behavior can feel like a drug. You get a rush or a thrill, you come down, and you look for the feeling again.

What kinds of feelings does risk-taking give you? We have heard kids say that risk-taking gives them **a feeling of being alive, a sense of power and control, feelings of being on top of the world**. Other kids say that it is a way **to express yourself, a way to belong to a group, to feel large, an opportunity to be heard and to not be ignored, a chance to not be a loser**. Ask yourself if any of these things are true for you.

Sometimes life can beat us down. We know we are young, but we feel old, tired, and hopeless. Things get so bad at home and school that we try to cut off from the negative feelings those places bring on. It's like a part of us dies. We become walking zombies. When we take a risk, it feels like a spark is lit inside of us. We feel alive again, even if it's only for a little while. We *think* we get in touch with our real selves. We might feel like we're ruling the world. Then when we get the negative consequences for the actions, we go back into the dead zone. We cut off again. We go back to being zombies. So, we start to crave more and more risk so that we feel alive and connected. The problem is that we get sucked into the cycle of risky behavior.

The Cycle of Risk Taking—
What Goes Up Must Come Down

Risk taking can cause us to experience many emotions depending on the type of risk we are taking and where in the risk-taking cycle we are.

Robert started stealing when he was about 12 years old. Mostly it was clothing, sneakers, and CDs. But then he got into stealing cars—for a bigger rush. He and his friends would scope out cars in the neighborhood that were easy to hot-wire. Late at night they would break in and cruise around. They would pick up friends who were impressed that they "had the balls" to steal cars. While they were driving around they felt pumped up. A couple of times Robert got caught. Then he didn't feel so high or large. His mother would get really upset because he broke the law again. She was sick of bailing him out and having to go to family court. Then Robert would feel like he let himself down and hurt his mother. He felt bad about himself. He'd wonder what was wrong with him. Then he'd feel himself shutting down and tuning out so he didn't have to listen to his mother make him feel guilty and stupid. Pretty soon, he wanted to take another risk to escape again.

16

DURING THE RISK
hyped-up
in the zone
paranoid
large & in charge
tough
alive

BEFORE THE RISK
bored
scared
nervous
sad
lonely
depressed
high
betrayed
edgy

The
Cycle
of Risk

AFTER THE RISK
scared
lonely
worried
paranoid
regretful
(shouldn't have done it)
let yourself down
let your family down
stupid
tense

Once you are aware of these triggers, you stop being a high-risk robot. You are . . . **FREE TO CHOOSE**.

Notice how the feelings at the beginning of the cycle and at the end are a lot alike: mostly negative. This is what keeps the cycle going.

Your Risk-Taking History

I been into so-called "high-risk" behavior since I can remember. When I was real little I started sneakin' money outta my mom's purse for candy and shit like that. After a while I would steal from stores if I didn't have the cash for what I wanted. By the time I was 13, I was buck wild and I'd be holdin' people up for their cash or jewelry. Now I'm serving a sentence for being an accomplice in an armed robbery. Sometimes at night when I'm sittin' in my cell, I think, "How did I get here?" But when I look back to all the shit I done and startin' so young and all, I get my answer.

Doug, 18 years old

Some of you might have been involved in high-risk behaviors for a long time. Maybe you started by taking small risks like jumping subway turnstiles or sneaking into the movies. However, as time went on and these things stopped giving you the same kind of high, maybe you moved on to more serious things. Maybe you got slicker and better at pulling things off and the stakes got higher.

✋ **Stop and Think:** When you look at where you are now, do you see a pattern of high-risk behavior? If you're in trouble with the law now, is this the first time that you have been arrested? Were there other crimes that you didn't get caught for? Is your risk taking getting bigger as time goes on?

High-Risk Sex: Are You Having It?

High-risk sexual behaviors are sexual acts that put you or others in danger. They can include a lot of things such as "forgetting" to use condoms, using drugs to make the sex feel more intense, having many partners, or having sex for money. High-risk sex can also include forcing a person to have sex against their will or coming on to them when they are too drunk or high to make a real decision.

 Stop and Think: When you look at your own sexual behavior, do you see more healthy or high-risk sex? How well do you get to know a person before you get involved sexually? Are you more willing to become sexually intimate than emotionally intimate? Do you have a habit of using sex to avoid painful or negative feelings?

Invincibility—Playing with a Loaded Gun

Part of the thrill or high you get from risk comes from the possibility that you might get caught. But another part says that there's no way you'll get busted. Maybe you think you're too smart or good at talking your way out of things. A small voice says, "It'll never happen to me." When you feel like your high-risk choices, decisions, and actions can't hurt you, it's called feeling **invincible**.

Believing you're invincible can make you feel powerful, tough, slick, large, and free from the rules that apply to other people. It can also limit your ability to see things for how they really are. When you're in the rush of a risk, you feel invincible and untouchable. You feel a false power. But that rush goes away fast. All of a sudden, you find yourself left with the consequences of your actions, whether or not you actually get caught. And if you do get caught, you begin to lose many of your choices, your power, and your control.

Feeling invincible does not mean that you actually are invincible. It is an illusion. It's not the way things really are. Feeling invincible tricks you into doing things that bring on more trouble. Invincibility doesn't last long. When the smoke clears, the high of invincibility vanishes, too. Ask yourself, Did I feel invincible after I got caught?

Getting the Screw-It Attitude

If you go around the high-risk circle enough times, you might develop a Screw-It attitude. It goes like this. "I'm so screwed now, it doesn't matter what I do. Since I'm in so much trouble anyway, I'm gonna do whatever I want to do. It can't get any worse or they can't give me anymore punishment than I already have…so screw it."

We've all been there. But here's the problem. *This kind of thinking gives away more of your power, self-respect, and dignity. No matter how deep you're in trouble, you always have the choice to change your behavior.* You will still probably have to serve the consequences for past high-risk behavior, but losing the "screw-it" attitude can get you out of the high-risk-taking cycle.

Take a deep breath and remind yourself:

**No matter how many times I've messed up,
I have the power to make better choices.**

Chapter 2

So Who Are You, Anyway?

"Who am I?" Well, that depends on where I am. When I'm chillin' with my crew, I'm all thug. When I'm kickin' it with the shorties, I'm one hundred percent player. When I'm at church with my granny, then I'm sweet and clean. So I guess you can say that who I am depends on where I am.

Earl, 18 years old

Will The Real_____

Please Stand Up

For a long time I didn't know who I was. I wanted people to like me so I was always doin' what I thought they wanted. Actin' in ways to be accepted even though I did things I knew was wrong or just plain stupid. I was always the one who would steal the smokes or beer if we had no cash. People could tell I was insecure so they took advantage of me. I would get in a lot of trouble for other people, and that made me feel worse about who I was. At that point in my life I felt like a real chump. It took a long time until I realized that I was just as good as everybody else. But once I did figure that out, I didn't get played so much. I didn't try so hard to get people to like me. I didn't need to because I started liking myself. The more I knew the real me, the more I liked myself and the less stupid shit I did.

Richard, 19 years old

So Who Are You Really?

Ever really asked yourself the question, *"Who am I?"* Male? Female? African-American? Hispanic? Asian? White? Native American? Angry person? A loyal friend? An honest person? A gang member? A thug? A dropout? These may be a part of you, but are they the *whole* story? Do these labels say who you *really* arc?

 Stop and Think:

Take a minute and ask yourself, WHO AM I REALLY?
Then write your answers here.

I am_____

I am_____

I am_____

I am _____

I am_____

I am_____

I am_____

I am_____

Are You Just Who They Say You Are?

As we grow up, we are constantly getting messages about who we are. If you hear you're a delinquent or good-for-nothing, you'll probably start to believe it. **But is that really who you are?**

Playing an Act: Are You on Stage?

It's not always easy to know who we are. And actually, that's your job right now, to figure it out. Sometimes we confuse the acts we play for who we really are. Maybe you have a reputation as an athlete, a druggie, tough girl, or a player. You may have played an act or worn a mask for so long that it even feels like that's who you really are.

You might be thinking, **"What ACT?** That's who I am." But take a minute and think hard and honestly about this. Let's say that an act is how you behave with others because you want to fit in or because that's how you've acted since you can remember. We may take on roles because of things going on in our families, like violence or alcohol abuse. We might take on a false self that is tough, harsh, or cruel to make ourselves feel protected. After a while, it is easy for us to believe that this false self is who we really are.

Dealing with adolescents in a prison is very difficult because everyone wants to prove themselves to each other because of the fear of being run over. Here at Madison, it seems like everyone walks around wearing a mask, including most of the guards. This is because no one wants the other person to know who he really is. You might think a person is real mean and bitter, when inside they are as nice and passionate as a baby. It's real hard to get to know the person inside because all you see is the mask, which is hatefulness and resentment. Therefore, you are either scared or don't know how to approach the person because of the image he's portraying.

I'll never forget the time I broke straight through a guy's mask. He was one whom everyone knew not to piss off, and it really didn't take much. Everything had to go his way or he would see that it went no way at all. He was one of those "my way or no way" type of guys, and he was very up front about it. I remember one morning we went to chow. The guards decided that everyone had to wear their coats to breakfast because the weather wasn't warm enough to wear a regular shirt or jacket. Disturbed with having to wear his coat, he argued with the guard. Once I saw he was done arguing with the guard, he walked past and got a drink of water, then sat at the table across from where I was sitting.

He said, "What's up?" in a very dark, deep voice. I played as if I didn't hear him. And then he said, "I know you heard me talking to you." At this time I looked up and said, "Oh, I'm sorry, Good morning," with a half smile on my face. He replied, "I said, 'What's up,' not good morning." Surprised with his response, I asked, "Why do you talk to me in such a tone of voice?" He said, "You wouldn't understand. I have a lot on my mind." With me anxious to know what's causing this guy to be so bitter, I asked, "Would you like to talk?" He got up, came over to my table and began telling me his problem. He explained he got 15-to-life in prison and it's been causing a lot of stress on his mind. I told him I was in the same situation. He couldn't believe it! He asked me how I dealt with my problems. I never seem to go off on people and blow up on people like him.

I began to tell him that I take it one day at a time and that I pray and ask God to give me the strength to make it day by day. To get this much out of this guy was very shocking because all I ever saw of him was the mask of the tough guy, not the hurt inside his heart. A lot of people in here have been misunderstood by the administration, communities, and families. I thought prison was a place where there was nothing but mean, hateful-looking monsters. I've met a lot of people that are totally opposite from what I thought.

Sedrick, 17 years old
(serving time in an Ohio adult prison)

Some people identify with a role or mask because they feel nothing else is there. But there is a danger in living an act. If you think of yourself as a gang banger, you will live that lifestyle. Violence, stealing, and revenge might start to feel like part of your nature, but they are not.

Emotional Phases — Is This Forever?

I was just mad, mad, mad, mad, mad, mad, mad all the time. I was one mad m*********. If you even looked at me the wrong way I would be all over you. I was mad so much that I didn't think there was anything else. For most of my life, being mad was being me. Then I learned that there was something more than my anger. I saw that anger was just a part of who I really was. The more connected I felt to the real me, the more calm I felt. Just remembering that I was more than my anger would help chill me out. I saw the anger come and go, but the real me was always there.

Ron, 18 years old

Are you like Ron? Do you feel angry so much that you think that's who you are—just an angry person? Or have you been really depressed or sad for so long that it starts to shape the way you see yourself and the world? Strong emotions can pull us in. Because they are so powerful, we confuse how we feel with *who we really are*. But even the strongest emotion will pass by. Sometimes if we are very depressed or angry we might need help getting past the emotion. But no emotion can ever describe all of who we are.

Am I More Than My Actions?

Take a minute to ask yourself these questions: Is anyone really born into the world as a bad person? Is there really such a thing as a bad seed? Are people who make selfish choices, get hooked up in crime, or hurt others really *bad human beings*?

The answer to those questions is **NO**. But there are some important things that need to be said before we go on. First, it is important to understand the difference between "who you are" and "what you do." This can be tricky because they seem to go together. We are taught to look at our behavior to figure out who we are. "I must be a loser because nothing I try ever works out" or "I must be a b**** because I yell and scream at everyone." For a minute, try to keep these two things separate. **BEING** and **DOING** are two different things even if it doesn't feel that way.

Our point is simple: No matter how bad a thing you have done, that is not who you really are. Let's say that you robbed a gas station. Does that make you just a thief? If you've lied or cheated, are you just a liar and a cheater? Absolutely not. Because within you is a power and wisdom that exists no matter what. Because within you is your true Self.

But, one thing needs to be spelled out before we go on. . . . No matter what, you are responsible for your actions. If you damage or hurt someone or something, *that's on you*. You are responsible for that behavior, no matter *why* you did it.

Your Basic Goodness

Everyone is born into the world as loveable and good. **Everyone.** When people treat us in a safe and loving way, it is much easier to keep connected with our basic peacefulness and goodness. When we are hurt, ignored, and disrespected we do things to survive. We do things to get attention, help, or get the things we want. And some of those things we do aren't so pretty. It can seem like our goodness isn't there.

But no matter what you have heard, nothing can destroy the basic goodness of your true nature. No matter how many times you screw up, hurt someone, or get hurt—your goodness can't be undone. It can't be erased. Your goodness is permanent and **real**.

The True Self

There is something deep within you that is the **real you**. When we talk about the real you, we will use the word Self with a capital S. Other names for the real you are **greater Self**, **true Self**, or **core Self**.

To get what we are talking about, think of a time when you felt deeply and strongly connected to who you really are. We're talking about something **truer** than any role you play or act you do or emotion you feel. Maybe it was a time when you fell in love. Some people feel this way when they do the right thing. Or maybe it was during a time when you were just watching the sunrise. Whatever the circumstances, you got a sense of your true Self. You felt connected to a deep sense of calm and peace.

Tuning in to the Core Self

You might say to yourself, "I never feel that way. I never feel peaceful and powerful." And that's because it is easy to get *disconnected* from your true Self. Sometimes we lose the station and just get the static. But that doesn't mean the station isn't still there. **By tuning into Self, you will be connected to a kind of power and wisdom that no role or act will ever give you.** The goodness of the Self is permanent. And just like with a radio station that comes in crystal clear, you know when you hit it.

Because your core Self is wise, patient, kind, creative, and loving, it will never steer you in the wrong direction as long as you are open to listening to it. It doesn't depend on what others think. It's much deeper than that. It's free from the noise we sometimes listen to when making choices. It's free from the hype of the money and glamour culture we live in. It's our real source of power and control over our lives.

What's at the Core

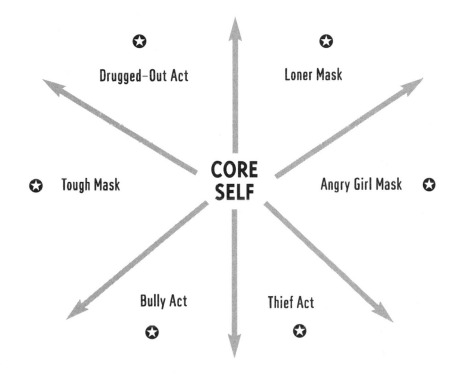

Take a look at this picture. At the center is the core or greater Self. This is the real you—wise, loving, kind, and good. It *never changes* and it can't be destroyed.

The little circles on the outside of the wheel are the acts, masks, or emotions that we sometimes get hooked into. These things are not permanent. Maybe you use drugs now, but in a year you might be clean. Today you bully; tomorrow you decide not to intimidate people. The tough girl/guy might leave these negative acts behind. Maybe you realize that stealing isn't worth the price you have to pay. And the anger that has been eating at you— you choose to let go of.

Finding YourSelf in the Storm

Sometimes we get very lost. We start acting in ways that cover up the true power and goodness of Self. It can hurt to think of the things we have done. We start to feel bad about ourselves. Even at our lowest point, the Self remains as good, pure, and honest as the day you were born. You just have to get hooked back up with it. Here are some simple ways to do that.

1 Talk with someone real. Find someone you can be genuine with. The more real you are with them, the easier it is to feel the power and light of your true Self. Think back to that conversation or person when you need to feel the power of Self at another time when you are in doubt.

2 Do something good, honest, right, or trustworthy. By doing something that has the same tune as the things that our Self is made of, we get back in harmony with who we really are.

3 Exercise. Sometimes working out really hard can quiet the mind down enough so you can hear the voice of Self again.

4 Meditate. It brings us back to the inner peace and power of Self. Chapter 14 gives directions on how to meditate.

5 **Be in nature.** No matter where you live, there is almost always a park nearby. New York City, Boston, L.A., Houston, Chicago…they all have them. Or if you live in a rural area, then maybe you are surrounded by nature. Look at trees, the sky, the earth. Feel it—get grounded. Breathe this energy deeply into your body. Remind yourSelf that the power and beauty of nature is the power and beauty of you. If you are locked up or you can't get to a place in nature, imagine it.

6 **Tuning into God or Your Higher Power.** For a lot of people, praying reconnects them to their true Self.

7 **Take time to remind yourself:**

No matter what, my core goodness can't be destroyed.

No matter what you have done, the goodness of Self is forever. This is a basic truth.

Chapter 3

Anger: Dealing With It
(Even if You Don't Feel Like It)

If we asked people reading this book what they thought their biggest problem is, most of them would say anger. And that's no surprise—because when we don't manage it, anger can rule us. At worst, it can destroy our lives and the lives of others.

Being angry doesn't have to be a problem. It's a human emotion that everyone feels from time to time. It's what you do with your anger that can cause problems for you and other people. Even if you haven't been on top of controlling your anger in the past, you can learn to control it now.

Finding out What Triggers You

The first step in getting control is figuring out what your triggers are. Lots of situations can provoke anger. What triggers or provokes your anger? Maybe someone shoves you on the basketball court. Or you hear someone say something negative about you or your family behind your back. You might learn that someone is trying to cut in on your boyfriend. Maybe a teacher punishes you for something that you didn't do. Whatever it is, we all have triggers. As long as you live in this world, your anger buttons will be pushed sometimes.

Here's a list of some things that might trigger your anger. After each one, put a number from 1 to 10 saying how much that thing triggers you. *Not all things should anger us the same amount.*

HOW ANGRY I GET:
1 = kind of mad
to
10 = very angry

TRIGGERS:
Someone steals something from you ____
Your parent breaks a promise____
You get blamed for something you didn't do ____
Getting interrupted ____
Someone gives you a dirty look ____
Your boyfriend/girlfriend plays you ____
Someone disrespects you or a family member ____

People spreading rumors about you ____
You get bumped into on the street and the person
doesn't apologize ____
Getting nagged ____

How often is your anger triggered? Once a week? Three times a day?

The Anger Fuse

Think of a stick of dynamite with a lit fuse on one end. The longer the fuse, the more time you have to put it out before the dynamite blows. **The more you understand your triggers, the longer your anger fuse will become.**

Stop and Think: On a scale of 1 to 10, how long would you say your anger fuse is now? (One is a quick temper and ten is a slow way of responding to anger).

Once I really went off on my mom. I got so angry that it was kinda freaky. I was feeling sick with like a cold and me and my sister were not getting along that day. My sister wanted the window open and I didn't. So after a while I turned on this little heater, but the air was getting on her leg, so she comes over and hits me. I hate hitting my sister because she's younger than me, but she just got me so

36

pissed that I slapped her in the face. She stayed quiet for about five minutes and then she started screaming that she was blind. I was feeling so scared and so sorry for what I did. Then my mom comes running in and asks what happened. I was so in shock that I just yelled that I hit her. Then my mom starts screaming, "You *****ing keep your hands off her, you *****ing b*****!" Now I'm *****ing heated and I start illin'. "Well, if you disciplined your daughter I wouldn't have to do it for you." Then my mom hit me in the mouth and I start bleeding. At this point I want my mom and sister to die a horrible death. I could feel my brain start pounding real hard like it was going to blow apart. My heart was beating mad fast. Tears were rollin' down my cheek. I felt like beatin' them both down and makin' them feel hurt like I did.

Monique, 14 years old

Anger in Our Families or "Do as I Say, Not as I Do."

The people in my family handle anger by screaming, fighting, and crying. You could say that they handle it with violence.

Lisa, 15 years old

When most people in my family gets angry, they scream and yell and talk shit to the person who pissed them off. Except my dad. When he gets mad, he gets real quiet. His face like stone, givin' you the silent treatment—then you know there's trouble.

Marquis, 16 years old

How we deal with anger is something that we learn. We learn it from watching our parents and the adults around us. We learn what is okay and what is not. Our parents let us know ways that we are allowed to express our own anger and ways we are not. Sometimes parents tell us to act one way but then they act completely differently. Maybe your brothers were allowed to scream, hit, and punch walls when they were angry, but you were not because you are a girl.

Watching our parents express their anger can be a confusing and frightening thing. This is especially true if their anger is directed at us.

Joaquim was an eighteen-year-old guy in one of the groups we run. He said that he once watched his father (who was about 6 feet 7 inches tall) hit an old woman on the street and knock her to the ground. She had accidentally run over his father's new sneakers with her shopping cart. Joaquim also had a tough time controlling his anger. He remembered feeling confused and ashamed of what his father had done, but he was too afraid to ask him about it because he was afraid of getting hit himself. In our group, Joaquim frequently said he had inherited his anger from his father and that there was nothing he could do to change his fate. Over time he came to see that he had much more control over his behavior than he gave himself credit for. As he became more aware of his anger triggers and the meaning that these triggers had for him, he gained greater control over his anger.

Stop and Think: What were the anger styles of people in your family? How did your dad express anger? Your mom? Do you express anger like the people in your family?

No matter what your parents' anger style is like, it doesn't have to be yours. Part of becoming an adult is deciding how you want to express your anger. Learning to deal with your anger in a positive way will take patience and practice. There will probably be times when you don't get it totally right. But the choice is yours.

Anger Styles

We all know that people have different anger styles. Understanding what your anger style is will help you get more control over how, where, and when you express your anger. Look at the list below and see if any fit you.

Hot Head - Explodes easily and is always on the edge of becoming angry

Silent Type - Shuts down and is real quiet once they become angry

Cold Shoulder – Won't deal with the person who made them angry. Cuts off from them.

Long Fuse - Can take a lot before they get angry, but then flips out

Pass the Buck - Keeps anger hidden from the person who triggered her and takes it out on someone else

The Waiter - Hides the anger during the conflict, but gets revenge at another time

The Faker - Pretends that they are not angry

The Masker - Hides their anger in humor or another emotion

The Stewer - Thinks about something for a long time before working up into anger

The Blamer - Blames someone else for making them explode

What Your Anger Feels Like

As you probably know, anger is not just something that exists in our mind. It is a powerful emotion that affects our bodies as well. People who experience high levels of anger on a daily basis are more likely to get sick and live shorter lives.

In fact, anger messes with our bodies' chemistry and balance. You might have felt some of the physical changes that happen to your body when you are angry: *a racing pulse, sweaty, clenched fists, tight jaw, breathing gets faster and more shallow, vision gets narrow like you're looking into a tunnel, get dizzy or lightheaded, muscles tense.* When some people get extremely angry, they cry.

Stop and Think: Where do you feel anger in your body?

Checking out the Scene: Is There a Threat?

Sometimes we think we are being **threatened**, but we're not.

Sometimes we think we are being **punked**, but we're not.

Sometimes we think we are being **disrespected**, but we're not.

This is important! If you always think that every look or word is a reason to "throw down," you might find yourself fighting way more than you need to. If you had to learn to read danger signs so you could protect yourself in dangerous places, *now you need to learn when things are not a real threat.*

Stop and Think: As honestly as you can, ask yourself if you sometimes misread people. Do you see a threat where there isn't one? Do you react to things with too much force? Think of a time in your life when you thought you were being threatened, challenged, or attacked when you really weren't. How did you react? Consider the *possibility* that you thought you saw a threat when there wasn't one. How would you have reacted if you read the situation correctly?

A Volcano of Anger

If you have a very short anger fuse, you might think that you are reacting only to the situation in front of you when you're not. Chances are, your anger is like a volcano. Over time, the pressure, the poisonous gases, and the hot lava build up. When one more ounce of pressure is added to the volcano, it explodes and burns down everyone and everything in its path. Even if you heard the volcano thing before or if it sounds corny, it's really true. Now ask yourself, where did this volcano come from? It depends on the person you are and what you went through before you got to this place.

People who are abused, kicked around, disrespected, or neglected usually build up a lot of anger inside. You might even find yourself blowing up at really little things. **Anger that is easily triggered and that is uncontrollable is rarely just about the situation in front of you.**

Think about a time when someone called you a name and you exploded into a rage. A reaction like this is probably because of the anger volcano that has built up inside. If your father or foster mother slapped you around, hit you with a belt, and put you down, you probably couldn't do much about it. Each time this happened, more anger, hurt, and fear would get dumped into the volcano. And now when anyone disrespects or threatens you, the volcano erupts.

If the volcano inside of you weren't already so hot and filled with pressure, some guy calling you a name wouldn't be enough to set you off. If you weren't already at the boiling point, you might just say "screw him" or "what's his problem" and walk away.

So How Angry Are You?

Think back over the last few weeks. How many times has your anger gotten out of control? How many times do you wish you could "undo" something your anger got you into?

As a person, would you say that you are:

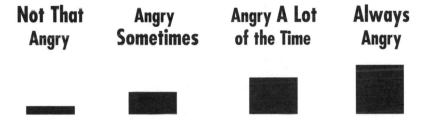

Not That Angry **Angry** Sometimes **Angry A Lot** of the Time **Always** Angry

When Anger Is Not Really Anger

Sometimes we think we are feeling anger when it is really something else. Many times, **there are other feelings going on underneath the anger**. These feelings can be left hidden for years because you didn't even know they were there. You thought you were just really angry. Other people thought you were just really angry. But probably there was more going on.

This is especially true for young men. In our culture young men are taught some stupid things about anger. You are taught that anger is tougher, cooler, and more manly than feeling sad, disappointed, depressed, or other "soft" emotions. Then when you turn all your emotions into anger, you are told that you are too angry, violent, and aggressive. And if you don't learn to deal with the real emotions that are going on—the emotions under the anger—then you probably will walk around feeling angry all the time.

You might feel anger so much of the time that you start to think that it's the only emotion that you have. It is certainly the loudest emotion. It takes up the most time and energy because it can be so hard to control. Next time you get really mad, ask yourself...*It might look like anger. It might feel like anger. But is it anger?*

Ronald's day was a real bummer. He went to court and the judge extended his stay at the detention center. Ronald's mother was supposed to show up in court to be with him, but she didn't. This started him thinking about all the times she let him down. Then he started thinking, "Why me?" When he got back to the detention center, the other kids start giving him crap about coming back. The tension in his body got tighter and tighter. He felt like a cork ready to explode out of the bottle. Finally, the last straw came when some kid got in his face at dinner. Before he knew it, he was on top of this guy, punching his face. Right before he started hitting, a small part of Ronald knew that he would pay for this later with restrictions and maybe a longer sentence, but he felt he was in too deep. He was just like, "screw-it."

Maybe you've even been in Ronald's shoes. You go to court, no mom, sentence extended. You might think you are just plain angry. But what feelings are deeper? **Frustration** that you have to stay longer? **Sadness** and **disappointment** about your mom? **Humiliation** or **shame** when you are teased by the other guys?

Each time we chose to only hear the voice of our anger, we become deaf to the deeper, more genuine feelings

44

fueling our anger. In order to heal and to really get control over our anger, we need to shift our attention. We need to allow ourselves to take off the anger mask and see what is underneath.

How exactly do you do this? Often you can figure out what these deeper feelings are by noticing what you were feeling *just before the anger struck*. Chances are you were feeling frightened, hurt, or in pain. Look closely at the clues. Did you feel threatened? Did you feel shamed or rejected? What were the deeper feelings that tripped off the anger? Dealing with these more genuine feelings is like going to *the source of your problems*.

Stop and Think: Take a minute and think of a time when you felt angry. Try to really remember what was going on at the time and how you really felt.

Now take a deep breath and go deeper into your feelings. What's going on underneath your anger? Were you feeling sad? Insecure? Helpless? Powerless? Hurt? Abandoned? Were you feeling the disappointment of a dream or expectation not coming true?

Look even deeper. What would have made the anger go away? Would having felt respected, loved, cared for, or given safety made you feel less angry?

If you cannot think of any other emotion that was going on at the time except anger, that's okay. But come back to this exercise later and try it again.

45

Expressing Your Anger

If you have ever lost it like Ronald, you're not alone. People express their anger in many different ways, but fighting is often the only way we know how to deal with conflict. Even if we tell ourselves we aren't going to do it this time, we slip back into old ways when we get stressed.

So what do we do? We might feel we've got to express our anger or we'll explode. Venting our anger can allow us to feel a sense of release and calm. But when we release our anger in destructive or violent ways, it's a problem. And it often comes back to haunt us.

✋ Stop and Think: How do you usually express your anger?

Unhealthy Releases

There are two basic **unhealthy** ways that we express our anger—outward or inward. We can turn it outward by **fighting, ignoring** someone, being **abusive or manipulative,** or **destroying someone's property.** Or we can turn it inside of us by being **depressed, hating ourselves, eating too much,** or abusing ourselves through **drugs, dangerous sex,** or **hurting ourselves.**

You might express anger in **sneaky** ways so that you are acting out your anger but it's hard for other people to put their finger on what you're doing. People who are sneaky-angry might act nice to teachers who anger them, but "pay them back" later. Or they might say that things are cool with a friend, but "forget" to invite them to a party. Basically, you try to keep things looking good on the outside, but release your anger in slick ways.

When I was growing up, my parents taught me not to show anger. If I had showed any anger at any time, I would have been beat up. So I was wise to keep my anger inside and never to talk about it. The way I got my anger out was by cursing my parents out in silence or sometime taking it out on my brothers or cousins. As I got older, withdrawing from everyday problems, from everybody, and using drugs were other ways I coped with it.

Hector, adult prisoner

Releasing It Safely

One of the best ways to deal with your anger is to think about something else or do something else until you cool down.

Don't let your brain get stuck going over it again and again. Switch gears.

There are safe and healthy ways to let that anger energy out. See which ones work for you.

Exercise - Exercise reduces stress. Playing basketball really hard and turning your anger into physical energy works for a lot of people. You could also go running or do sit ups, or lift weights.

Talk out Your Anger – Find someone who you really trust and talk it out with them. Share your true feelings about the situation. Find someone who will listen without judging you. Then let it go. If it feels safe and right, try and talk it out with the person you're angry at.

Writing - Write about your anger. Write about everything making you angry. Keep writing until you have all your feelings down on paper. Some people like to write their angry feelings down on paper and then rip it up into a thousand tiny pieces.

Music and Dance – Turn on some upbeat music as loud as you can and dance. Or don't dance. Sometimes just having music pulse though your body can really change your energy. But be careful what you listen to. If you put on angry music, chances are it will take your mind to that negative place.

Meditation – Taking time to focus on your breathing when you are really angry can stop anger in its tracks. It can also give your mind the space it needs to deal with the problem in a more creative way. (Chapter 14 tells you how to meditate.)

✸　　✸　　✸

Stopping Yourself in the Moment

My anger gets me into trouble a lot. But there was one really bad time when I got an assault and battery charge. What happened was this girl was talkin' shit to my sister and she wouldn't stop. When I told her to stop, she told me to mind my business. The things she was sayin' was so disrespectful. Nobody is gonna disrespect my family and get away with it. So that's when I hit her and my sister hit her and we really f***ed her up. We beat on her so bad that she got permanent damage in one of her eyes. I got locked up for five months for that. It's still hard for me to control my anger, but it's a lot better now. I've learned how to walk away more.

Erica, 15 years old

Perhaps the hardest thing to do when you are angry is stop yourself before you do something dangerous, violent, or destructive.

You probably know the Nike ad "Just do it"? Well, it's the same for anger management. Do not give yourself any other option. **Force yourself to chill.** Make up your mind and get it done.

Don't let snapping be an option. Bring the freight train to a screaming halt. Put your whole mind behind it. For that moment, stopping yourself is your only job in the world.

The steps below give you the valuable seconds or minutes that you need to think of a better solution to your anger. Following these steps will give you the time to ask yourself what you really need to do to keep your power and control. It will get you out of the crisis and into a place where you can release the anger safely. If you are in the habit of snapping when you get mad, these steps will take practice. But ask anyone who feels the power of controlling their anger and they'll say that the practice is worth it.

Stopping the Anger in Its Tracks

Stop - The first step to getting control in the moment of a conflict or a fight is to make yourself stop dead in your tracks. You can do this by imagining a big red stop sign. Or pretending to hear a siren or alarm go off. As you feel the anger start to rise, use your body signals as a clue. Is your temperature rising? Are your fists clenching up? Sometimes it helps to do something physical as you tell yourself to stop—like take a really deep breath. This reminds your whole body to stop before you act out the anger in a dangerous, out-of-control way.

Remind Yourself – You have a choice. No matter how good you think it might feel to let your anger go by punching this person, there will be consequences that will not feel good. Remind yourself that by expressing your anger through violence or aggression, you hand over your power. . . to the person provoking you, to the cops, the judges, and the wardens. Try and get your mind off it. Go do something else.

Am I Reading This Right? There is the chance that you have misread the situation. Do you see a threat where there isn't one? Do you hear a put-down when no one has even spoken?

Back off While Still Saving Face – You don't have to look like a punk to leave a conflict without fighting. Find a way that works for you. You don't have to play into someone by getting pulled in to his/her anger or game. Sometimes it just takes walking away into another room.

IMAGINE YOU ARE WATCHING SOMEONE COOL WALKING AWAY FROM A BAD SITUATION WITHOUT LOOKING LIKE A LOSER. THIS PERSON HAS FOUND A WAY TO KEEP THEIR POWER BY CHOOSING TO STAY CLEAR OF TROUBLE. IMAGINE THAT THE PEOPLE WATCHING ARE IMPRESSED BY HIS ABILITY TO WALK AWAY WITHOUT LOOKING LIKE A CHUMP. IN FACT, HE SEEMS LIKE HE IS **ABOVE** THE WHOLE THING. HE SEEMS IN CONTROL, ON TOP OF HIS GAME, AND SMOOTH. THIS GUY LEAVES THE CONFLICT FEELING TOTALLY IN CHARGE OF HIMSELF. NO ONE WAS ABLE TO SUCK HIM INTO A PLACE HE DIDN'T WANT TO GO. HE FEELS GOOD. IMAGINE YOURSELF ACTING THE SAME WAY.

Release Your Anger Safely – If the energy from the anger is still in your body, choose a way to release the anger in a way that works for you.

Give Yourself Credit – If you can walk away from a situation that triggered you without fighting, congratulate yourself. How do you feel? Can you feel the power in your self-control?

Stopping yourself in the moment of anger can be hard to do. Very hard. Making the choice to stop can take practice and time. Be patient. If you stick with it, it will become easier and easier each time you chose to stop.

Our Anger, Our Choice

When you hold on to anger, it's like saying to another person, "Here, you can have my power. Here, you can have my happiness. I'll just give them to you." If you are angry at a person, imagine walking up to them and saying that. Sound ridiculous? Well, if you're holding on to your anger that's exactly what you're doing.

Each time our anger is triggered, we have a choice. We can throw gasoline on the fire by the things we tell ourselves. Or we can chose to cool ourselves down with calming thoughts and anger management tools. In the end, it's a choice you make. It's a choice about real power. Remember, anger sucks our energy and power away from us. Nobody feels good walking around angry. You might fool yourself into thinking you do. But try feeling in charge of yourself for a while and you'll never want to go back.

Chapter 4

Relaxation—Finding Peace When the World Feels Crazy

When my mom is on my case, it really stresses me. She's always naggin' me about this or that. I can't even walk in the house without her bustin' on me about school or askin' me where was I. Sometimes I feel like my brain is going to explode.

Stan, 16 years old

We are all human. And because we are all human, we all experience stress. All kinds of things can stress us out—problems with friends or families, school, trouble with the law, being alone, or even riding a crowded bus. When we are very stressed, our breathing might become faster and more shallow. Our muscles tense up and we can feel like we want to explode. Our minds might race and we might get caught up in negative or destructive thinking. Sometimes our stress might not be so dramatic. We begin to feel more anxious. We keep going over the same stressful thoughts. Our minds become like broken records playing the same words over and over.

Because we will never live in a stress-free world, we need to develop ways to reduce our stress *no matter where we are.* If we don't find ways to release this tension in healthy and responsible ways, we run the risk of snapping. Or we just feel bad and ground down by life. One of the best ways to manage or "tame" our stress is to learn how to relax. When you relax deeply and let go of stress, it's like you turn down the noise in your head. Then you can hear a deeper wisdom guiding you—the voice of your core Self. Even if you are on a noisy cell block with people screaming and the TV and radio blaring, relaxation gives you the power to become more peaceful and calm without having to change your environment. Real relaxation comes from within.

You might be thinking, "I already know how to do that. When I need to relax I grab a beer (or a joint) and watch TV." While these things might feel relaxing to you or allow you to chill out, there is a deeper kind of relaxation. It is a kind of relaxation that you can use anytime and anywhere. We are talking about a kind of relaxation that helps you **quiet your mind**, but still lets you be **aware, present, and focused**. Watching television just creates more noise in your head. And although drugs might seem relaxing and take the edge off your negative thoughts, they actually work to numb you. Real relaxation allows you to be **centered and peaceful** without shutting down.

Relaxation is also an attitude that allows you to remain calm even in the middle of stress and confusion. Relaxation moves you out of the winds of the tornado and into the center where it is quiet and still. **Relaxation is not about being "laid back" or fronting an attitude that nothing bothers you when inside you feel tense, anxious, or upset.** When you're really relaxed, you feel good. You feel more alert and alive. You feel more at peace with yourself and the world around you.

Relaxation Techniques: Finding Power in Peace

Just like anything that requires skill (like basketball, playing the guitar, or driving a car), relaxation requires that you learn the moves and practice them. Of all the relaxation techniques, becoming aware of your breathing is the biggie. As for the rest of the techniques, some might feel more natural to you than others. Try them out and see what works for you.

Breathing

There is a powerful connection between your mind, your body, and your spirit. Whenever your mind becomes stressed, you might also find that your breathing becomes rapid and shallow and your muscles become tense. Becoming aware of your breathing pattern is one of the simplest and most effective stress-reduction skills that you can learn. Simply by breathing deeply and evenly, muscles relax and thoughts become quieter and calmer. It's like taking control of a car that is speeding out of control by first taking your foot off the gas and slowing down. Breathing is like your body's gas pedal. It regulates your mind and body. It can help determine how fast or slow you go.

Daily Reminder

As you go through your day, remind yourself to breathe fully and deeply. In general, the deeper you are breathing, the more relaxed you will be. *The next time you find your body tense up when you are in a stressful situation, take four deep breaths* **before you do anything else.** In fact, you don't have to wait until you're stressed. Do it anytime.

Deep Belly Breathing: Paying attention to your breathing

Put both hands on your belly like you're holding a basketball. Breathe in deeply through your nose, letting your stomach muscles expand as far as they can. Your hands will move out like the basketball is getting pumped up with more air. Next, exhale through your mouth, letting your muscles contract. Let out a sigh as you exhale. The basketball should deflate under your hands. Feel your facial muscles, shoulders, and the rest of your body relax as you exhale. Repeat several times. Try this now.

Breath Counting

Breathe in to the count of 4, breathe out to the count of 4. Imagine breathing in a peaceful energy as you breathe in to the count of 4 again. Breathe out to the count of 4 and feel your body relaxing. Feel your muscles relax as you breath out. Then at the same speed, breathe in to the count of 8 and breathe out to the count of 8. Again, breathe in to the count of 8 taking in a peaceful energy. Then, out to the count of 8 letting your muscles relax. Then breathe in to the count of 12 and out to the count of 12. And in to the count of 12 and out to the count of 12.

Then stop counting and enjoy the fullness of your breathing.

Self-Talk and Breathing

Repeat a word or phrase that helps you relax. For example:

Inhale and as you inhale, say to yourself: *"I am…"* Exhale, and as you breathe out, say to yourself, *"calm."* As you say these words, feel your mind let go of stressful thoughts. Let your muscles let go of tension. As you continue to repeat these words with your breathing, let your breathing become deeper and slower. Try this for three or four minutes. If you find your attention wandering, gently bring it back to your words and breathing. Let yourself enjoy the feeling.

Body Scan and Breathing

Scan your body. Notice how different parts of you are feeling. As you inhale, imagine you are breathing clear, soothing, healing energy into the areas that feel tired, painful, or tight. As you exhale, imagine the tiredness, the pain, and the tightness leaving with the breath.

Scan your entire body from your toes to your head. Breathe in a soothing, calming energy with each breath you take in. Breathe out tension with each breath going out. Go from one body part to the next. Start with your feet. Put all your attention on your feet. Imagine breathing in a soothing, calming energy, as if you were breathing in air directly from a really peaceful place in nature. Then breathe out and feel that part of your body relaxing. Feel the muscles relax.

Then, one at a time, do the same with your ankles, lower legs, knees, thighs, the lower part of your body, your stomach, lower back, along your spine, chest, upper back, shoulders, arms, hands, fingers, neck, jaw muscles, face, forehead, and scalp.

Then bring your awareness to your entire body and breathe in the peaceful energy for a while longer.

Positive Visualization

Images in your mind have an immediate and deep effect on your physical and emotional state. Have you ever woken from a frightening dream and found your heart racing, your muscles tight, your fists clenched? Even though you were in a safe place and the scary events from your dream weren't actually happening to you, your body and emotions reacted like they were real. Your nervous system can't tell the difference between what is happening in real life or purely in your imagination.

In the same way, if you imagine relaxing and peaceful experiences, your body doesn't know that you're not on a beach in Jamaica or walking in a beautiful park. When you visualize yourself feeling relaxed and confident, you are programming yourself for physical health, success, and positive emotions. Basically, visualizing means that you are deciding what kinds of images, movies, or pictures you want in your head and playing them. Think of a computer. By deciding which disk you pop in, you control what shows up on the screen. It works the same way with your mind. If you visualize peaceful and relaxing images, your mind and body will react by becoming calmer.

Peaceful Scene

Take a few deep, relaxing breaths. Feel your body become more relaxed and less tense. Then, using as many of your senses (for example, seeing, hearing, smelling) as possible, imagine yourself in your perfect place for relaxation. Be as specific as possible. For example, if you are walking on a beach, what color is the water? Is the water warm? Can you feel the sand on your feet? You don't have to have actually been to a beach in Jamaica to have this visualization. One of the most powerful tools that we were born with is our imaginations. Or maybe there's a place like your grandmother's house that makes you feel calm and relaxed. You can smell her cooking fill the house and hear her voice in the kitchen. Outside it's cold and raining, but inside it's warm and comfortable. Take a minute to remember a place like this.

Daily Life Scene

Take a few deep, relaxing breaths. Then, using as many senses as possible, imagine yourself calm, clear, and confident moving through your day. Feel the good power that is always inside of you. Imagine feeling this way in a potentially stressful situation. See yourself in control, relaxed, and totally able to deal with whatever comes your way.

❋   ❋   ❋

In a way there is nothing new about the things that are written in this chapter. Of course we are breathing all of the time. Your body will breathe whether you remember to do it or not. Just remember to breathe a little more deeply from time to time. When you are aware of your breathing, you can use it as a tool to bring peace and relaxation into your body and mind. It is a tool that you don't need to buy, it can never be taken away from you as long as you are alive, and it is with you all of the time.

It is a powerful and effective way to bring peace into your life fast.

And just like we are breathing all of the time, we are telling ourselves things, too. There might be a CD playing in your head all the time and you might not even know that you put it on. It might sound something like this: "I can't do it." "I'm not good enough." "It's always gonna be this way for me." Sometimes how you feel is just a matter of the CD you pop into your head. We can choose to let the negative stuff play loud or we can get in touch with our peace and power. *The choice is up to you.*

Remember to breathe and consider this:

Within me there Is a peacefulness
that cannot be disturbed.

Chapter 5

Families:
Where We Come From

The only reason I turned to the street is because my family didn't understand me. My father was never there for me. He went off and never took responsibility for me and my family. I want my son, who is now two years old, to see the world differently. To have what I never had. I want to show him that there's a world out there for him beside the street corner and gang life. I want to show him that gang life doesn't make you a man. I want him to know that education, a good home, a family, and friends are the key to a happy, successful life. I'm going to give him the kind of family that I wanted but never had.

Mark, 19 years old

In order to figure out **how you got to this place**, it helps to look at **where you come from.**

No family is perfect. Even the family that looks perfect has its own struggles and challenges. But for some people, their family could not provide the very basic kinds of emotional support and safety that kids need. Maybe your family had to deal with a parent who was in jail. Maybe there was violence in your home. Or maybe your mom or dad was out of the picture and you grew up in a string of foster families. Whatever the deal was, we hope that some of the sections in this chapter speak to you and your family experience. In the next chapter, we'll deal with how drugs and alcohol affect families.

Families almost always trigger powerful reactions in us because they are some of the most important experiences in our lives. Families shape how we feel about ourselves and how we see the world. Many of you might still be going through a lot with your family right now. We hope that reading this chapter (and the book) will help you feel more at peace about your family life, even if you cannot change what goes on in your home. By healing some of the emotional wounds now, you might not have to carry them around for years to come. **And most importantly. . . the better you understand the patterns and history of your family, the more power you have to break cycles of unhealthy behavior.**

Can the Apple Fall Far from the Tree?

I always hear that I'm just like my dad, especially when I'm mad or being stubborn. My dad can be really harsh, and to outsiders he looks scary and mean. He has made a lot of mistakes in his life. Bad choices. I have really tried not to be so much like him. . . but sometimes it's hard. I want people to see me for who I am. Not just to see me as being just like him.

Sara, 16 years old

Some of you might have heard the saying **"The apple never falls far from the tree."** Other sayings mean the same thing, like: **"He's a chip off the old block" "They're cut from the same cloth"** or **"Like father, like son."** What do these expressions mean to you? For most people, the point of these sayings is that you end up acting like your parents or the people who raised you. That brings up some big questions. If your family members made bad choices, does this mean that you have to follow in their footsteps?

A lot of times we look at the people in our families and see that people all have the same color eyes or a love of music. Sometimes we see a pattern of addiction to drugs or alcohol, fathers not raising their children, or people getting involved in bad relationships. Although these patterns might be true for the past, they do not need to predict the future.

One young man named Tony told us about how his mother used to throw hot water on him when she was really mad at him. Every time she did this, she would scream that he was a "no-good piece of shit" just like his father. Tony grew up believing that his dad was bad and he was bad too. The way his mom made it sound, Tony had no choice about it. She made it sound like he was born bad because of who his dad was. But as Tony got older, he learned he had the power to make his own choices—no matter what choices his dad made.

Take a deep breath and repeat these words:

No matter what my family has been through, the strength and power within me can never be destroyed.

Histories of Abuse and Neglect

Talking or even thinking about abuse or violence that happens in the home is no picnic. Many people try to close the door on those memories and never bring them out into the light. But as you may have figured out already, the hurt and pain we suffer in our homes does not just magically vanish by not thinking about it. We can try to run from those memories or shut them out by drinking or drugging—but often they stay around like shadows hanging over us until we face them.

Experiences of abuse and neglect shape the way we see ourselves. And those memories color the way we deal with new relationships. It is possible to leave painful pasts behind us to clear the road for a loving and peaceful future. But first, you need to heal the pain in order to really let it go. Be patient. Healing the pain of abuse can take time. It usually doesn't happen overnight. But just by reading this chapter you have made a great start. Give yourself credit for being strong enough to do that.

As you read this chapter, it is important to remind yourself that any abuse in your home was not because of who you are or what you did. No matter what happened in your family, kids *never* deserve to be abused, neglected, or harmed in any way. If this happened to you, no matter what you've heard, **it was not and is not your fault.** In a soft voice (even if it feels corny or weird) repeat the words: **I did not deserve to be hurt.**

Family Violence

The very first violence I witnessed between two people was between my mother and father. I couldn't have been more than five years old. I just remember him knocking her to the floor and all this blood rushing out of her nose. She started screaming and grabbed a knife. Seeing that made me feel unsafe, terrified, and unprotected. I felt like I was going to be his next victim. And if she couldn't protect herself, how was she supposed to protect me? Funny how things work, because I was next.

Miguel, 19 years old

In every family, people say things that they wish they could take back, tempers get lost, and there's stress. But for some families, things get really out of control. Some families get into dangerous cycles of physical and emotional abuse. This is one of the most frightening things that can happen in a family. It destroys the victims' feelings of safety and trust. It can make anyone who goes through this—especially kids—feel trapped, terrified, and alone.

David came from a very violent home where he saw his father beat his mother all the time. The abuse made David hate his father. He used to have fantasies about killing him for all the pain he put the family through. He wanted his father to know the same kind of fear and pain that his mom did. As he got older, David blamed himself for the violent things his dad did. His dad always said that David and his brothers getting into fights and trouble stressed him out and that was why he beat their mother. David also felt guilty that he couldn't protect his mother. He saw that his friends' dads didn't beat up their wives or girlfriends. Then he felt like a freak, like his was the only family in the world going through something this messed up.

Keep in mind that, although we have a natural instinct to protect the people we love, children (even teenagers) are never responsible for physically or emotionally protecting people in their family. You may have taken on this role in your family. If this is the case, don't go it alone. Call one of the numbers listed on pages 252-255 or find someone you trust to talk to. Protecting your family from violence shouldn't be your job—no matter how much you love them.

Keeping Secrets

I didn't tell anyone about the abuse in my house toward my mother and me and my sisters because I didn't think anyone would believe me. That's what living in such a screwed-up family does to you. You're so scared. Even though you're walking around with black eyes and fat lips, you think no one will believe that you are getting the shit kicked out of you. I was also ashamed about what was going on. My whole childhood was filled with feelings of shame and disgust about myself and my family. But the biggest reason I was afraid was that if I told, my father would kill us all. Once he put my sister in the oven and tried to close her in there when he thought she told about how he beat us. He was crazy. No wonder I was terrified to tell. Eventually, someone called the police and they sent my mother and us kids to a battered women's shelter. Like a safe house. It probably saved our lives. No, I'm sure it saved our lives.

Julie, 19 years old

If you come from a violent family, chances are you've tried to hide it. Living with secrets always takes a lot of

68

energy out of you—even if you are not aware of it. If you find yourself keeping secrets about the abuse in your house, try and get help. Domestic abuse is a bomb waiting to go off. Sooner or later someone could get seriously hurt.

Sometimes people even "keep secrets" from themselves and pretend that what is going on in their house is normal and okay. They try to convince themselves that seeing their mother or sister being threatened, beaten, or raped is just something your family has to deal with. You might say, "Hey, this is the way it has always been and we've survived so far." But don't be fooled. If you are living in a violent family situation, get help now. You aren't alone. Thousands of families in this country suffer from domestic abuse. Don't let your feelings of shame keep you from getting help. Get out of the danger by calling a hotline (see pages 252-255), telling a counselor, or speaking to another adult who can help you.

And don't let getting locked up be the way you get out of a bad place and get help.

Violence against Me

Many kids who get caught up in high-risk lifestyles have been the victims of physical and emotional abuse. The abuse could be from your biological parents, foster parents, relatives, or stepparents. Most of you know what we mean when we say abuse, but let's just go over it quickly so we're on the same page. *Abuse is any act that hurts, violates you, or puts you in danger.*

Physical abuse comes in the form of hitting,

punching, kicking, burning, and other acts that could seriously hurt another person. Usually the abuser is larger and stronger than the victim, but not always.

Emotional abuse is when people use words or looks to injure others by making them feel stupid, useless, scared, or in danger. Emotional abuse also includes leaving kids alone for long periods of time before they are ready to take care of themselves. Things like throwing out someone's clothes as punishment and not buying them the food or medicine that they need (when money is available) are forms of abuse. When kids are not supported, loved, cared for, or when they are left to get the things they need for themselves, it is called *neglect*. And while it might not seem as bad as being hit or punched, it can cause just as much pain and suffering.

Sexual abuse happens anytime someone who is more powerful than you gets you to engage in sexual behaviors. Sometimes someone older takes advantage of you sexually, but you agree to it. This is still sexual abuse. Sexual abuse can include kissing, touching sexual parts of the body, intercourse, and oral sex. Even if the sex felt good to the child (and it sometimes does), it is still sexual abuse.

Even being shown pornography as a young kid or having people make sexual comments about you is sexual abuse. This can make you feel guilty and like "you asked for it." Remember, an adult never has the right to sexually touch a child or teenager. **No matter what you did or how you felt,** you are not responsible for the abuse that you experienced.

It Happens to Guys, Too

Although many people believe that only girls and women can be the victim of rape or sexual assault, this is not true. Many boys and young men have been victimized in this way. You might be ashamed and afraid to get help to deal with your feelings about being sexually abused. You might be afraid that what happened to you means you are weak, homosexual (if you aren't), or damaged goods. **None of these things is true and you are not the only one who has had sexual abuse happen to him.** Just as with any form of violence or abuse, sexual abuse is extremely traumatic for the victim and can even be more confusing and terrifying than being beaten or robbed.

If you have been the victim of sexual abuse, it is important that you reach out for help. You are not alone. It happens to guys more than you might think.

Discipline or Abuse?

Ever been told that you were the worst, most hard-headed, most disrespectful kid in the world? Well, even if these descriptions fit your behavior, it didn't mean you deserved to be abused. We'll say this over and over because you might not believe it deep down. Maybe you needed some serious discipline or rules, but never abuse. There is a big difference between discipline and abuse. Discipline means setting boundaries (or limits) and guiding your child to learn right from wrong. You might not like discipline, but all kids need it. Children who are disciplined learn that the world is safe and fair. There are rules. If you break them, there are consequences.

Abuse is taking out your rage, anger, disappointment, and frustration on your children. Children who are abused learn that the world is dangerous and cruel. They get the message that they are useless and not worth protecting. They begin to see themselves as damaged goods. Remember, being abused does not mean that you are really any of these negative things, even if that is the message that got sent to you.

How Abuse Affects Kids

Maybe you don't even think of some of the things people did to you as abusive. Or maybe you know for sure that you weren't treated respectfully and you're angry. People have different reactions to abuse and neglect, and all of these feelings are legit. The real point of this chapter is helping you deal with your emotions and discover your strength—no matter what has happened in your past.

Your Emotions

I was sexually abused by my uncle since I was seven. I don't remember exactly how it started with him touchin' me. He was always buyin' me presents and tellin' me how I was his special angel and what a beautiful girl I was. The abuse went on for a long time. I knew it was wrong, but part of me felt like it was my fault for lettin' him touch me. So

I kept quiet. I was scared to tell. He said that it would kill my mother if I told. He said that she wouldn't believe me and she would throw me out on the street. And he said that nobody would want me after they found out that I let him touch me. I felt dirty and kinda sick in my stomach. I blamed God for letting this happen. I thought my life was ruined and that nobody would marry me if they found out my secret. It's been some years now, but it's still hard for me when I think about it. Sometimes I get angry about what he took from me. How he could do that to a little child? Thanks God I have people who believed me and helped me.

Marta, 16 years old

Some of your feelings might be really intense at the time of the abuse, like extreme fear for your life, rage, numbness, shock, and terror. These feelings might change over time. Many remain long after the abuse has stopped. Others might not come back until years later as you have your own children or see your abuser again after a long time. You may have felt some of the following feelings at one time or another: **shame, fear, anger, resentment, frustration, hopelessness, used to it, ruined, loneliness, humiliation, like you deserved it, like you didn't deserve it, confusion, rage, regret, disappointment, confusion, unfairness, sadness, and disbelief**.

My whole childhood I felt scared to death. I never felt f***in' safe. I felt terrified all the time. I was always anxious, never knowing when I was going to be punched in the face, spit on, or back-handed for laughing at something. Every day felt like it would be my last. Six-year-old kids are not supposed to worry about dying. But I did. I felt worthless. I could never do anything right. I felt a lonesome emptiness and helplessness. I hated my face, my eyes, myself. My whole life I felt weak and with no confidence. But mostly, on an everyday basis, I was scared to die. I had nightmares. I was in hell.

Steven, 19 years old

Some kids ask, "Why me? What's wrong with me that would cause this to happen." The answer is No matter what happened, the abuse was not **because** of you. It was about your abuser. Physical, sexual, and emotional abuse happens because your abuser was not able to deal with life in a healthy way for whatever reason. It is not because there is something wrong with you.

Take a deep breath and repeat these words:

No matter what, the abuse was not my fault. And the goodness within me can't be destroyed.

How Abused Kids Sometimes Act

Here are some stories of how other abused kids acted.

Even though Mark was smart, he had trouble in school because he couldn't concentrate or pay attention. It felt like his mind was always somewhere else. He had problems with almost all authority figures who reminded him of his abusive father. By eighth grade, Mark was skipping school most days.

* * *

Pilar found it hard to make friends because she didn't want them to find out about what was going on in her house. Although closing herself off from people seemed like a safe choice, it left her feeling lonely and isolated.

* * *

Shawanda was physically and emotionally abused by her mom and stepfather. For most of her life she had a history of getting involved in high-risk behaviors. The thrill she got helped her feel more in control of her life. She also did drugs and drank to forget what happened to her at home and to be "pain-free" even for a short time.

* * *

Ricky acted out the anger and violence he experienced at home on those around him. He abused others to feel powerful.

* * *

That Never Happened to Me

At first it might even be hard for you to admit to yourself that you were the victim of abuse. It is often too painful to believe that the people we most want to love or the people we are counting on (like our parents or grandparents) could hurt us.

When you look back over your childhood, sometimes it is really clear that your parents actions were abusive, like if they hit you and broke bones. Other times the ways we were hurt are harder to pin down or point to. But these less obvious kinds of abuse (like being ignored, made to feel stupid, or abandoned by your parent) can be just as painful. These require healing too.

Why Should I Have to Think about This?—The Past Is the Past!

If painful things happen to you as a child and young adult, like being abused, witnessing family violence, watching your parents do drugs, or seeing them go to prison, **you are more likely to get hooked up in those things yourself**. Many times people who have been a victim go on to be a victimizer. This doesn't mean that *you have to* or *are going to* do these things; it just means that you are at *greater risk*. Understanding these cycles helps you break out of them.

Dealing with painful parts of our past can be hard. But there are often serious consequences if you cope with your past abuse and neglect by using high-risk behaviors.

Going to jail, getting sick, or hurting others are a few examples. Although talking about what has happened to you might seem like a more difficult way of dealing with your problems than getting high, it offers you a way to heal and let go of the pain in a much deeper and more permanent way. It offers you the chance to be free at last.

Our Responses to Trauma

Trauma is a fancy word for what we go through after something **really** painful, frightening, or upsetting happens to us. (Think of being in the World Trade Center during the terrorist attacks and escaping. Or having someone you loved die because of the attacks.) But trauma can come from things that are way more common than terrorism. **Anyone who has been severely abused or has witnessed (seen) a violent act against another person has probably experienced trauma.**

Because trauma is so personal, there is no one way that people feel or deal with it. **Any feelings you have because of a trauma are legit and okay.** People who have experienced a trauma like sexual or severe physical abuse may feel intense fear or horror. They might also feel numb. The traumatic event might keep popping into your brain over and over even when you don't want to think about it. The traumatic event might cause you to have nightmares or have trouble sleeping. A lot of kids who experience trauma act hyper or like a motor is driving them. It's almost like they can't slow down. Some people block out or "forget" the trauma and don't deal with it at all. These are all normal reactions to trauma.

Am I Nuts?

Some people feel like the abuse they experienced wasn't real, almost like it was in a dream or it was happening to someone else. It can make you feel separate from your own body. Maybe you start laughing when you talk about the abuse you suffered. You might feel like you are going crazy. This is especially true for kids who tell that they are being abused, but no one believes them. Or maybe you tell and your abuser denies it and says you are making it all up. This happens a lot with sexual abuse—especially if your abuser is someone in the family or a close friend. It is often hard for a mother to believe that her husband, brother, cousin, or friend could do such a horrible thing. **You are not crazy.** You know the truth, and there are people who will believe and help you.

Trauma does a real number on our brain. And with any deep wound, it takes time to heal from traumatic events. Trauma is a natural response when we have experienced abuse, violence, or have seen someone else experience them. It is often difficult to talk about these events. Our brain tells us to avoid them so we can avoid the painful memories. But this is only a short-term solution.

When traumatic things happen, we need to deal with them at our own pace. The process of healing or recovery is different for everyone. At times you may feel relief—like you're really making progress. Other times you might find yourself reliving painful old feelings.

This is all part of healing and recovery, and it's all hard work.

Usually, our mind will only let out the memories that we are ready to face. That way we don't get too overwhelmed. Even so, when we really deal with the trauma in our lives, we might feel worse before we start to feel better. Don't let this stop you. The reward of working on your pain is that eventually it fades away. But if you do start to feel overwhelmed, talk to an adult you can trust. Again, you can call one of the hotlines on pages 252-255. You can also try some of the exercises in the relaxation and meditation chapters (4 and 14).

The first step to dealing with trauma is knowing that you have some healing to do. Although you might be able to do some of this work alone, we recommend that you talk to a therapist, a teacher you trust, a social worker, or any wise and caring adult. If this isn't possible, talk to friends who have been through the same thing. Talking about your feelings is the best way to release them from your mind and body. Healing the wounds of abuse is key to gaining your freedom, peace, and power.

Take a deep breath and repeat these words:

No matter what, the goodness and power within me can't be destroyed.

Family Incarceration

Sometimes when families experience drug and alcohol abuse, violence, or criminal acts, jail becomes part of the family. Anyone who has been through this knows: **Having a close family member in jail can feel like everyone is serving the sentence.**

Sometimes you might not even know the truth about where your parent is. Some kids don't find out that their parent was in prison until much later. Many families try to protect kids from the truth by telling them that the parent went to the hospital or is away visiting relatives. You might hear things on the street, but you might not really know the truth. If your family hid the truth from you, they probably thought they were doing the right thing to protect you. But being lied to can make the whole deal worse.

I didn't want to know the truth about why my dad went to jail. I'm pretty sure that he killed someone in a fight. Me and my pops, we don't talk about it. My social worker takes me to visit him, but I asked her not to talk about that in front of me. I mean I had heard things. It had to be pretty heavy because he got life. People in my family keep saying he was framed. I want to believe that. But no matter what my dad did, he's still my dad and I love him. He's a good man. I know he worries about me. He sees me getting into trouble now and he doesn't want me to wind up in prison. It's even worse him being in there because he feels like he can't guide me and teach me the ways of the world.

Tony, 16 years old

Over time many kids do learn the truth. And many kids decide they want to see their parent in prison. If you have a parent in prison and you want to visit them there, maybe you can find a relative who is willing to take you. If you have never been to a prison before, the first time can be hard. It can bring up a lot of concerns about your parent's safety and well-being. Allow yourself to feel whatever comes up. Ask questions and talk to your parent about your fears. Visiting becomes easier over time.

Susan's Story

I have been in and out of the California prison system for most of my adult life. In between my sentences I had two beautiful and intelligent children. Sometimes when I look at them and see how well they do at school, I wonder how in the world they came from me.

Over and over I tried to kick my drug habit. And over and over I would let myself and my children down by relapsing. It always happened the same way. I'd stop showing up for work, then I wouldn't report to my probation officer. Next thing I'd quit going to family gatherings. But the worst was when I would cancel my visits with my children with some lame excuse about why I couldn't show up. The real reason was that if I was with my kids, I couldn't get high. Taking care of my children became the last thing on my mind when I was high. As much as I truly loved them, the drugs didn't leave room for anything else.

So, back to prison I would go. A place I knew all too well. Old friends would greet me with a cigarette and I would catch up on prison gossip about all the home girls. Soon the drugs would wear off and the first thing I start thinking about is my children. Reality hits and I can't believe that I've let them down again. Now all I want is to hold them in my arms. Sitting in my cell, tears run down my face. I wonder who my children are with and what they are doing. Other women are getting mail and pictures from their loved ones, but nothing comes for me.

Then one day I get a letter from my 13-year-old daughter. And this is what it says:

Hello Mom,

How are you doing? I got your letter today and I just needed to let you know a few things. **No one** stops me from writing to you. I haven't written to you in so long because I can't stand to repeat things I've written to you in the past so many times before. Mom, you always say that you're not going back to prison and that you will never use drugs again. You know, Mom, I just feel so let down. I'm starting to think that you actually **like** prison because you keep going back. Is it because there you have no responsibilities? No one to take care of? Is it so that you don't have to deal with your problems or the mess you have made on the outside?

I think that you turn to drugs with the thought that they will solve your problems. Have drugs solved your problems so far? Mom, when are you going to realize that real life is not about drugs and prison? It is about doing your part as our mother. Next week I am going to graduate from junior high and you've chosen to sit in jail instead of on the bleachers like everybody else's mother.

Sometimes I feel like I don't even have a mother that I can turn to with my problems, happiness, or pain because you are always running back to prison. My brother and I are so hurt and disappointed. All we ever wanted was to have our mother here with us like the rest of the kids. Why do you keep doing this to us? Do you think we'll just wait for you forever and let you into our lives anytime you want so you can let us down again?

Mom, I'll never stop loving you, but this is getting old. And so are my brother and me. So the next time you think you have it hard, think again. Because me and my brother are motherless.

After I read that letter, it changed me forever. I sat down and wrote my children a long letter apologizing for what I had done to them. I explained that my problems had nothing to do with them, even though they were the ones who paid the biggest price. I got involved in a twelve-step program that helped me deal with my addictions and now I am in recovery. I realized that I had to stop feeling sorry for myself and take responsibility for what my life had become. Even though I am making changes, I feel like I can't promise them anything. I have broken my word too many times. I have to show them with actions. It's a long road, but I'm going to keep walking until I find my way. I just thank God that they were willing to give me another chance. Despite all of the disappointment I have caused them, I think they can see the love I have for them. A love that drugs could cover up but never destroy.

When the Anger Gets Turned against the Cops

Feeling angry at the police when someone in your family is arrested is natural. The word may be that your parent was "framed" or "set up." Almost everyone wants to believe that their parent is innocent and doesn't deserve to be in jail. Or perhaps you have had your own negative experiences with the police and feel that there is no way that cops could act fairly.

If this is true for you, it is important to make sure that your beliefs don't place you at great risk if you have contact with police. The organization 100 Blacks in Law Enforcement gives presentations across New York informing kids how to respond if they are ever stopped or detained by the police. The most important advice they give is to stay calm and not make the situation worse. **_Keep your cool._** If you are walking around with an enormous amount of rage toward police, it could easily escalate a situation and bring on more trouble. In the end, you pay the price if you turn your anger against the police.

The Legacy of Prison

There is a strong connection between having a close family member go to jail (or prison) and winding up there yourself.

In my family every male goes to prison at the age of 16. And I mean everyone. My dad, my brothers, my two uncles, and now me. It broke my mother's heart, too, when I went. And then she was just like, "Well, he's just like the rest of them." I don't even know how it happened really. It's just like a curse.

Chris, 16 years old

You might not think that jail is cool, but there may be some powerful things in your life pulling you there. Here we aren't just talking about your high-risk behavior, but some of the deeper thoughts and feelings about who you are, what your family is about, the type of future you will have, and how you fit into society. Many young men have told us that almost every man in their family has spent time in jail at one point in their lives. Because of this, they begin to believe that they will go to jail too. Some young men see their futures as so hopeless that they don't see jail as any worse than life on the street.

Stop and Think: Take a minute to think about how you see prison. As honestly as you can, make a list of both the positive and negative things about prison. Do you see yourself gaining anything by going to prison? Do you see yourself losing anything?

In general, people don't plan to go to prison. They don't sit down and say, "Hey, you know what? I think prison will really work for me. I'm going to get busted this afternoon!" Unfortunately, they don't plan *not* to go either. No matter how many people in your family have been incarcerated, *prison does not have to happen to you*. No matter how bad your neighborhood is or harsh your home is, you do not have to go to jail.

No matter how badly you have done in school, you have choices. The power that you have lies in the moment-to-moment choices you make. You can choose friends with bad reps or ones who will do the right thing. You can get involved in street life or you can help out in your community. There is no magic pill or potion. Each day and each moment offers the opportunity for power, dignity, and peace. *Choosing to stay out of jail is in each of these small moments.*

When Home Is Not an Option— Foster Care

My mother left me with my aunt when I was a child. My father left me never to return. Not having my mom present when I needed her made me feel alone. Sometimes I wished she walked through my aunt's door, but that never happened. I believe that's when I started to get real angry in my childhood. Acting out in school and not listening to no one. I hated the world for giving me parents who showed me no love.

My father only lives in the next city. I always pictured him showing me how to handle tough situations and protecting me. Not having any parent to show you the world or how to love or feel. No one to protect you when you scared. No one to show up and ask you how you feel. It made me feel vulnerable, like I was all alone in dark woods trapped. I felt like I couldn't get out of situations or face challenges or make my own decisions. I became angry, confused, and desperate looking for someone to love. It led me to a lot of negative and risky behaviors in life.

Jerome, 18 years old

We almost never meet kids who *want* to leave their homes. No matter how bad things get because their mom, dad, or grandparents were drinking, drugging, or being violent, almost nobody wants to leave their things, their school, their bed, and move into a total stranger's house. Even if you are moving in with a relative, sometimes there really isn't enough room or you just don't feel at home. Home might be bad, but at least you know what to expect.

And many kids say that the abuse they suffered in foster care was much worse than what happened to them at home. (Of course this isn't true for all kids. Some make life-long relationships with caring and loving foster parents.)

I got taken out of my house because the neighbors called ACS (child protective services). My father and mother was always fightin' and carryin' on. Sometimes they would go out drinkin' and leave us alone for days at a time. Me and my little brother got sent to this foster home. And there was too many other foster kids there. The older ones was always pickin' fights with my brother and stealin' from us. The foster mother didn't care. She didn't help us even when I told her. Once, our mother sent some money and clothes over for us, but the foster mother said she never got it, but we know she did 'cuz her own kids was wearing the clothes.

Shaniqua, 14 years old

What It Feels Like to Be in Foster Care

It's scary to go to a new foster home when you don't know anybody there. I kept thinking that somebody there wasn't going to like me and would try to fight me. I was also afraid that if somebody tried to fight me, I would get really mad and then I'd get kicked out and have to go back to OYS [lock-up]. I was one of the lucky ones to have a very good foster family. I thank God every day for them.

J.T., 16 years old

Waiting for Mom

Most kids in foster care spend their time thinking about when their mom is going to take them back-for good. Or maybe they are waiting for her to just visit.

In foster care I lied all the time about my mother. I'd make up lies to everyone about her coming to visit me and how she was getting ready to take me home. Or how I had talked to her on the phone last night (when I hadn't) and how she said that she had called to make sure that I hadn't been adopted because she was coming to get me. I would say that she wanted to make sure that whoever was in charge knew that I wasn't allowed to be adopted. All lies. Everything I said about my mother back then was a lie except that I missed her and that she was beautiful and that the only thing I wanted was to be with her.

Martin, 18 years old

Being placed in foster care might make you feel like there's something wrong with you. You might say, "If only I acted better my parents wouldn't have hit me. Then I would be at home." "If my parents really loved me they would stop drinking or getting locked up and come get me." It's natural to feel this way. It's also common to blame yourself for being in foster care. But it's not your fault. No matter what you did, it didn't cause your parents to drink, drug, steal, hurt you, or leave you. **Foster care is about your parents' inability to take care of you—for whatever reason.** And remember, foster care is not forever. Many people who have gone through the foster care system have gone on to lead happy and powerful lives. You have this option too.

Adoption

Being adopted was something real sad for me. I was 13 years old when I realized that my mother wasn't capable to take care of me because of her drug use. I called my aunt and asked her to adopt me so that DSS (Department for Social Services) wouldn't put me with strangers that I didn't know. When my aunt adopted me I went to Puerto Rico with her, and let me tell you, I felt so sad and lonely. Lonely because my mother and I was so close to each other. We shared our feelings with each other. And I was sad that I couldn't see her because I was in Puerto Rico and she was in New York. Now thanks God we are together again because she has changed her drug behavior. And the change is for the best!

Rosa, 16 years old

Not everyone is ready or able to take care of a child once they have one. Sometimes giving a child up for adoption is the most loving thing a parent can do. Most babies or children are placed in adoption because the parent wants a better life for his or her child. Some kids feel like it's their fault that their parent chose to free them for adoption. But it is not. **No matter why your parent decided that he or she could not take you back, it is not because of who you are.**

If you were placed for adoption without really knowing your biological parents, you might have a lot of ideas about what they were like and why they chose to place you for adoption. You might also have a lot of fantasies about what your life would have been like if you had grown up with your biological parents. You might think that your life would have been better, that you wouldn't have gotten into trouble, that you would have been loved more. Or maybe you feel angry at them for giving you up. You might also some day want to find your biological parents. This is an issue that is very personal. Give it some thought. Talk it over with someone you trust before you do it.

As you become more independent, you will begin making important decisions about your life for yourself. The more at peace you are with your past, the easier these decisions will be to make. The less you are ruled by the disappointment and sadness of adoption or foster care, the more power you will have.

Chapter 6

Drugs and Alcohol

In my house there was a lot of drugs and alcohol. My stepfather used to always hang out at the bars and my mom worked in one. They used to come home around three in the morning and get into these big fistfights. Telling me who is to blame for this and that. The fights between my mother and her husband were all over drugs and alcohol. Sometimes my mom threatened her husband with a kitchen knife. It would happen three or four times a week. My stepfather's family is all from troubled pasts and grew up on the street and in jail.

I brought my street life into my home and I was selling weed and coke to my stepfather. I even helped my own mother fall into that life of using coke. They never showed me love so I figured at the time, "Who cares?" I could make the money here in my own home. The problem was I felt like crap. I knew there was something wrong, but I ignored it. Then me and my step father started getting into violent fights where bats and knives would come into play. All this was over my anger that my parents were addicts. This is where my life became a real mess. I had no love. I felt torn and depressed. I had no sense of direction in my life.

Jesse, 17 years old

What Substance Abuse Does to a Family

Anyone who has lived in a family where someone is addicted to drugs or alcohol knows how it can ruin a family or at least hold it prisoner. Drugs and alcohol do not just affect the life of the user. They mess with the lives of anyone who relies on, lives with, or loves the user.

For a long time my mom was real messed up on booze. When she was sober, she was the greatest person to be with—real smart and funny and nice. But when she started drinking, she was nasty. She was like Jeckyl and Hyde— with two personalities. Sometimes she would go for weeks not drinking and we would be like, "yeah, maybe she kicked it." But then she would be gone for a few days and come back messed up and hidin' out in her bedroom. Once my friends saw my mother past out on the couch and they were cool about it and pretended not to see nothin'. But inside I felt ashamed. Why couldn't she just be normal like other peoples' parents?

Greg, 16 years old

Anyone who has seen a substance abuser knows that they have a physical need to get the drugs that their bodies have grown used to. These needs are so strong that they come before anything else. When people use drugs for a long time, it has a powerful impact on their body and personality. As substance abusers become more and more addicted, they have less control over their lives. Feeding their addiction becomes their main focus in life. Many kids have said that even when there was no food in the house, their parents always had alcohol and cigarettes. Kids get the message that their parent puts his or her own needs first and everyone else's needs second.

When Promises Get Broken

My father always promises to stop drinking. Every time my mother yells at him about it, he said that he's done with it for good. To me, when he is drunk he would promise me a lot of things too. One time he missed my birthday and promised he would make it up to me by taking me to get new rims for my bike. But he never did it. I never asked him about it because I didn't want to make him feel bad. I love my father, but really, his word doesn't mean anything to me when he's drinking. And that's most of the time.

Santiago, 16 years old

Deep down inside your parent may have really wanted to keep his or her promise. She wanted to stay straight, but without help, addictions are hard to break. So what does it feel like to have your trust broken over and over again? Well, for one thing, you might have a lot of anger toward your parent. You might feel that if he loved you enough, he would kick the habit. You might also find it hard to trust what other people say to you. You might think that everyone is going to let you down.

How It Feels to Live with an Addict

There's a lot of things I would change about my family if I could. But mostly I want to change my dad because he doesn't support us mentally or physically. I want him to use his money wisely and not gamble with it. Most of the time he gets his paycheck he takes it to the track and blows it. This really stresses my mom out 'cuz then there's no money for rent or food. We are always getting our phone and lights shut off. My mother is always screamin' at him about how selfish he is. She says, doesn't he even care about his kids not havin' the stuff they need? But he can't stop. He's a gamblin' junkie.

Juanita, 17 years old

For years, doctors, psychologists, and social workers have known how tough it is for kids to grow up in addicted families. One thing that almost all of these people point out is that many families in this country have to deal with the problem of addiction at some point. Sometimes it helps just to know that millions of kids have gone through many of the same things you're going through.

Living in an addicted house stirs up a lot of intense feelings for kids. Here is a list provided by a group of kids whose parents were substance abusers. Did they leave any out? Angry, ashamed, disappointed, sad, guilty, embarrassed, alone, tired, confused, frustrated, mad, like it's unfair, afraid, different than other people, scared, trapped, helpless, hurt, self-hatred, out of control, crazy, tense, edgy, hyper

More Secrets and Shame

Even when parents don't come right out and say it, many kids feel like it is their fault that their parents have an addiction. No matter what message you have gotten, **NO KID IS EVER RESPONSIBLE FOR THEIR PARENTS' SUBSTANCE ABUSE. EVER.**

Substance abuse in the family is usually something that people try to hide and keep a secret. When you feel like you're carrying a secret like this, it's like you automatically feel ashamed and guilty. This is true even if part of you knows that you didn't do anything wrong. Getting past these feelings of shame is important. Shame is one of the most poisonous emotions that a person can feel and it can have a powerful grip on your behavior. We'll talk about how to deal with shame later.

But no matter what has been going on in your house, breathe deeply and remind yourself:

No matter what my parents have done—it cannot destroy the goodness and power in me.

Denial

Many families don't even talk about the fact that someone in the family has an alcohol or drug problem. It is a fact that they live with every day but are silent about. When people get the message that they can't talk about their feelings, they either hide them or let them out in other ways. When people refuse to even admit that there is a problem, that's called **denial**.

You might have heard your parent say that they "could quit any time that they want," or that they only use "to have a good time." Sometimes we want to believe that this is true, because if they could control their drinking or drugging, then maybe they could stop. Unfortunately, addiction is a disease, just like cancer. And unless the person with the substance abuse disease gets treatment, they probably won't get control of their addiction.

If your parent is denying that there is a problem, it will be hard for them to get help. But that doesn't mean that *you* have to deny there is a problem. Even though the addiction is your parent's, you can get help. It probably won't change their behavior and make them stop using, but it can change the way you feel—about yourself, about them, and about your life. When you get help for yourself, you'll probably feel less alone and your life will feel less crazy. There are support groups in many places such as hospitals, community centers, on reservations, and in drug treatment outreach centers. Ask a counselor or see pages 252-255 of this book.

Roles

When families live under a lot of stress or have a lot of problems, people in the family sometimes take on different roles to deal with it all. Some of these roles include the *troublemaker, the clown, the rescuer, or the lost kid.* The roles that family members play take the attention away from the person with the *real* problem (the substance abuser) and put it on someone else. This helps the family deny that the substance abuser is the real problem. Sometimes the roles help reduce stress in the family by letting people focus on someone else's problems. Sometimes the roles help kids get the attention they need either through positive or negative ways.

Here's an example of how a role works. Say that your family role is the "troublemaker." You get in so much trouble that everyone is always busy worrying about what you did or what kind of trouble you're going to get into next. Because the spotlight is always on you, your mother doesn't have to take a look at herself and see how her addiction is affecting the family. So your troublemaker role keeps the real heat off of her and on you. The problem is that it keeps your mom from dealing with the real problem—her addiction.

My whole family got a lot of problems, but I mostly feel bad for my brother. He don't have the love he wanted and needed from my family. They abuse him and treat him awful. They blame all our family problems on him. Life is hard for him so the only thing that makes him feel better is taking drugs, smoking, and drinking. After doing all those things for a while, he started skipping school. I think his future looks very bad. I wish my parents would give him the love and support that he deserves, but they don't. Right now he's involved in so many fights. I'm afraid he's going to get killed. Everyone thinks that he's the bad one. Even though we all do bad things, compared to him we look good. My family are weird. They are afraid to show love. They always want to go against each other. I love my family, but they need a lot of help to change.

Sasha, 16 years old

Roles don't allow the person to be who he or she really is. When people are playing a role, it can be harder to hear the voice of Self. The role sucks you in. And the longer the person plays a role, the more the family depends on that person to keep playing that role so the family doesn't have to face the truth. This makes it very hard for people to grow into adulthood and become whole and healthy people.

Stop and Think: If you are coming from a family where there is substance abuse, is there a role you play? What do you think might happen in your family if you stopped playing that role?

Looking at Your Own Substance Abuse History

Learning the Ropes

One day I was chillin' with a girl that was four years older than me. I was twelve. She gave me some weed. Everyone in the room was smokin' and I didn't want to look like a little kid. I was afraid they would laugh at me or tell me to get lost. So I tried to smoke it without coughing too much. I didn't like it at first, but it made me feel kinda down with them. Later I used it more because it helped me lose my stress when I used it. I thought, "If my moms uses it, why shouldn't I?"

Latisha, 16 years old

Parents' drug problems can sometimes get passed along to their kids. There are a lot of reasons why this happens.

First, you spent a lot of your childhood watching your parents use drugs or alcohol. For some people, the first cigarette they smoked was their parents'. Or the first sip of beer they had was at one of their parents' parties. Even if your parents didn't mean to, they probably "taught" you about using just by you watching them. Even if you hated living in the house with a person who was dependent on drugs or alcohol, part of you might say to yourself, "if they like it or need it so much, there must be something good about it."

Other Reasons We Start Using

The first time I started using drugs was in the 7th grade. I guess I did it because I felt like no one in my family loved or trusted me. My parents never asked me about school or how I'm doing. I used the drugs to relax my mind so I don't have to think too much about what is wrong with my life.

Latrell, 15 years old

When I used to do drugs and drink, it made me feel older by having young kids look at me and see what I was doing. I thought I looked tough at the time.

Owen, 16 years old

Stop and Think: When did you first use drugs, sniff inhalants, or drink alcohol? What made you try it. What did you think afterwards?

Whatever the reason you started using, you got something out of it or else you would have quit. Maybe you liked the high or maybe you did it to be down with your friends. But whatever the reason, it gave you something that temporarily made you feel better, cooler, older, freer, mellower, more relaxed, less angry, or less sad. But when you're really honest, you can see what drugs took away from you.

While I was drinking I stopped concentrating in school. I just never went. And I didn't care less for my family and friends. I didn't listen to the people who care for me and was wanting me to stop. One time when I was drunk, my friend said something to me that I didn't like, so I threw her across the room and hit her a couple times. Then I walked away like nothing even happened. That's what drugs did to me.

Shaniqua, 16 years old

You should also know that smoking marijuana in your teenage years screws around with the way that your brain grows and develops. The part of your brain that plans about the future, understands the consequences of your actions, and makes choices is still changing as a teenager. If you're smoking a lot of marijuana, you are most likely decreasing the power of your brain. This is no joke. We know pot seems like no big deal compared to other drugs, but it is not as innocent as you think. Also, smoking a lot of marijuana makes it harder for your brain to make the juices that make you feel good naturally.

Over time, drugs might become the only coping strategy that a person has for dealing with conflict or negative emotions. If this is the escape hatch to your problems and you don't have any other tools to deal with them, chances are that you will always turn to drugs or alcohol to deal with your problems. Using drugs and alcohol to cope with your tough emotions or problems lets you escape them for a while, but the deeper feelings you are running from don't get dealt with.

The more you get caught up in using drugs, the more you lose touch with your core Self. Choosing drugs to run away from our problems leads us away from the power and wisdom of the deeper Self. And it is the core Self that has the power to help us deal with problems in a real way. Using drugs closes the door on our true strength. It keeps us in the dark.

Javier's story is a good example of a problem that led to negative emotions that led to him using marijuana to escape. Javier's problems in school started when he was in the fifth grade. School was hard for him and he found it boring and frustrating. When things got to be too much for him, Javier would act out and the teacher usually had to stop teaching in order to deal with him. He spent a lot of time in the principal's office, and his mother was called to school almost every week. This created big problems at home, and Javier was always losing privileges or being grounded. By the time he was in high school, Javier almost never went to school. He spent most of his time hanging out with other kids who were truant and smoking pot. Sometimes he would steal or deliver drugs for older guys to get money for marijuana and beer. Two times he was arrested for stealing. This made him feel worse about himself and more alienated (alone) from the people and places that could help him deal with his problems. Javier didn't want to think about his future because people kept telling him how hard it was going to be for him to make a living if he didn't have a high school degree. When Javier was high, he didn't think about feeling like a failure and a loser for basically dropping out of school. He also didn't think about how much he had disappointed his parents. However, when he wasn't smoking or getting drunk, he felt overwhelmed by his problems at home and school, and all he could think about was getting high to feel better and shake his fear and shame for a while.

Javier's story may sound familiar to you. Maybe your problem didn't start with school. Maybe it had to do with your family, or the abuse you might have experienced, or some of the high-risk choices you made. All of a sudden you might notice that you feel tense or angry all of the time. When we live with these difficult feelings like shame, rage, sorrow, or fear, it can seem like a heavy weight on our back. We're always looking for a way to get rid of this weight, even if it's only for a short time. In order to shake those feelings off or to escape them, many kids turn to drugs and alcohol.

What Triggers Me?

One way of better understanding your drug or alcohol use is to think about the thoughts or feelings that *trigger* you to use. Just like certain events trigger our anger, certain problems or emotions can trigger our impulse to use drugs or alcohol. For example, when you feel stressed out, nervous, ashamed, bored, or angry, are you more likely to use? What thoughts are in your head about your drug or alcohol use? Do you tell yourself that you deserve to feel better so why not get high? Do you tell yourself that everyone around you is doing it, so why shouldn't you?

When my friends have a party, it's hard for me to go and not drink. They use the "homeboy excuse" to make me drink. Even if you say you don't want to drink, they say, "Do it for your son, man. Do it for your homies." And they love to pressure you to drink so much that you can't do anything but knock down to the floor.

Phillip, 18 years old

You've probably figured out by now that the risk of us getting involved in unsafe or high-risk behavior becomes much greater when we're stoned or high. How many times have you done something when you were drunk or high that you wouldn't have done if you were sober? Is your behavior on drugs different than your behavior when you're straight?

I used to get high every day. I would hang with whoever would give me the drugs, I didn't care what kind of people they was. I did things I was ashamed of with guys to get the drugs. Then I got to the point where I was looking like an old lady with bags under my eyes. And I looked so dirty and smelling bad. It took a while for me to stop, but I finally did. And I'm not putting any more drugs into my body ever again.

Krista, 17 years old

If you are using drugs, it is difficult for you to live to your potential. Drugs cover up the power of your core Self. In other words, despite what you may think, you are smarter, stronger, and healthier when you're straight.

Stop and Think: Take a minute and think about your beliefs and attitudes about drug use. Then as honestly as you can, write down what you get from using drugs and what you lose. Don't just think about the

107

present, but picture your life six months, one year, and five years from now. Unless you really believe that drugs and alcohol will not work as a lifestyle choice for you, it will be hard to leave them behind.

Getting Help

At a certain point, drugging or drinking might become a hard core habit or an addiction. **Not doing it** might feel strange to you. You may be at a place where you don't realize how dependent you are on drugs and alcohol both physically and emotionally.

If you have a serious problem, you're probably going to need help to deal with it. At the back of this book you will find numbers for places that can help you to kick addiction problems. However, if you are still denying your problem, you probably won't decide to get the help you need. Many people have to bottom out before they will get help. Just remember, drug and alcohol problems only get worse with time. The sooner you do something about it, the easier it will be to deal with.

Chapter 7

The Lost Childhood

Many of you might look at where you are right now—in trouble with the law, secure detention centers, residential treatment centers, or jails—and wonder: "Man, how did I get to a place like this?"

We don't know exactly where you come from or exactly what you went through. But we do know that all of you are survivors. And most survivors have one thing in common. Most have the feeling that they never had a real childhood.

No Kids Play Here

Never having a childhood can mean a lot of different things. Maybe you couldn't go outside to play because you lived in a dangerous neighborhood. One 15-year-old guy told us that when he was a little kid he remembered looking out of his grandmother's window and watching other kids play basketball on the playground. His grandmother felt that his neighborhood was too dangerous and so she wouldn't ever let him out of the house to play with the other kids. He felt that being trapped inside all of the time was part of losing his childhood.

What Takes Away a Childhood?

Did family violence take away your childhood? Never feeling safe in your own house, constantly watching for signs that someone might cause you danger, or having to protect others from people causing your family members pain can also make you grow up fast. Physical, emotional, and sexual abuse rob kids of the feeling that they are safe and free from worry.

There are other ways to feel like your childhood was taken away. When parents use drugs or alcohol or are never around for you, kids have to take on more responsibility than they feel ready to. Sometimes older kids have to take care of their younger siblings (or your parents) and so they never get to hang out with friends. Some kids even have to go to work outside the home to help support their families.

Your parents might be around but be too involved with their own problems or activities to have much time or energy for you. Maybe they spend all of their time with their girlfriends or boyfriends or don't seem interested when you try to talk to them. This kind of behavior can make us feel unheard, unimportant, and lonely as well.

What? Grow Up? Are You Kidding??!!

Feeling that you have to start acting like an adult when inside you believe that you *never got to be a kid* can seem like a bad joke. It can make you feel cheated and pissed off. Mostly, it can seem really unfair that you have to start taking on the responsibilities of adulthood when you feel like you got robbed out of being a kid. It would be nice if we could stay young until we got all of the love, education, guidance, and support that we felt we needed to move onto the next phase of our lives, but unfortunately we do not. Yeah, everybody wants the privileges that come with adulthood, but that's different. What we're talking about is feeling like you got forced into adulthood before you were ready. Walking on a wire without a net. Getting shoved out of the nest.

Be a Kid? Man, I Have a Kid.

I had a baby real young. I didn't plan on it, but part of me thinks that I did it on purpose so I could have someone to love me. See, I never got that kind of love from my family. Having a baby seemed like a way to have someone to me with me 24/7. But now that I have a baby, it's different from what I thought. Yeah, it's 24/7, but that means always changing diapers, getting bottles ready. Being waked up like five times a night. I love my baby, don't get me wrong, but I'm doin' the givin' not the gettin'. That's for sure. It's hard too because I wouldn't say my mom was a good role model for how a mother should act. So I'm kinda trying to figure this out on my own.

Chantal, 16 years old

If you already have your own child, feeling like you got robbed of your childhood can seem even stronger. So now no one is taking care of you, plus you have to take care of someone else. When you are a parent, what you want and need comes after what your kid needs. You want a new coat, but there is only enough money for one coat? Too bad, because you know the baby comes first. At least, that is what it takes to think responsibly about your child's needs.

We have talked to lots of young women who believe that having a baby means that there will be someone around to love them. All their lives they have craved love and attention. But they didn't get it from their parents. It's like there is a hungry hole in the heart. So now the deep need to be loved tells them that a baby will do this. They think, "My parents couldn't love me, but this baby will. This baby will be *my real* family." And while this is true, they don't realize that a parent's love is *different* than a child's love.

The kind of love that you crave from your parents is all about being taken care of, nurtured, and supported. The kind of love you want is unconditional. That means that no matter how much you messed up, got into trouble, or said mean, nasty things to your parents, they would still love you. If your parents were mature enough to give you *unconditional* love, they could still see the perfect, loving, good, and wonderful you no matter what you did. But the kind of love you get from your child is different. A child's love will not satisfy those needs to be taken care of and nurtured. That is not what children do. That is not their job. And any of you who have been forced to be a parent to your parent know this is true. Bringing a child into the world to give you what you want or need is tricky business. And looking for your child to give you the love you crave sets up the child to lose their childhood just like you did.

Entitlement

Lost childhoods leave you feeling like you got the short end of the stick. A lot of you probably walk around feeling cheated or screwed out of what you deserved. Some kids tell us that they feel like they have a big hole in them or an emptiness that they are trying to fill up. If you feel that you were deprived of the things that kids need from their parents, you might feel that you have the right to make up for that *any way you want*. Maybe you feel like you deserve to get what you want by *any means necessary*.

113

My mother just had so many damn kids. There was six of us. I was always hearing, just wait until I get paid, then I'll get you the boots you want. I got so sick of hearin' that because every time that check came, I got the same thing—nothin'. And my friends were all walkin' around with hot gear. So then I just started takin' whatever I wanted from stores. I was like f*** it. Why should everyone else be wearin' good boots, and pants and fifty-dollar shirts and I'm wearin' this shit.

Marquis, 15 years old

The word that best describes taking or doing whatever you want because you feel cheated or you had a painful or difficult day, week, month, year, or life is entitlement. **Entitlement can play itself out in a lot of different ways.**[1]

For example, you might feel like it's okay to take from someone else because you think they have a lot and you never had much at all.

You might steal from your parents because you feel like they never gave you what you wanted.

Maybe you feel like you deserve to get drunk or high because your day was so bad that you have the right to feel good whenever and however you can.

114

> You might even justify forcing sex on someone.

Some people feel entitled to act violently toward others because this is the way that they were treated. "Hey, I've been through a lot; I deserve to lose it once and in a while."

All of these are examples of entitlement. And here's the big problem: **Entitlement often leads you to get what you want by violating the rights of others.** In the case of forced sex, you're screwing up someone else's life. With drugs or truancy, "entitlement thinking" can lead to high-risk behaviors that may have negative consequences for you.

When Entitlement Leads to Risk-Taking

Believing that life is not fair and feeling we're entitled to even the score can lead to high-risk behavior. Drugging, stealing, and having dangerous sex can all make us feel for a short time that we got what we wanted. It can make the wanting go away for a while. Or it can give us a rush or high that feels good. But all of these high-risk behaviors can have serious consequences and make us feel even worse and lonelier than we did before we committed the high-risk act. Remember the cycle of risk-taking we talked about in chapter one?

This last time I got locked up was because I stole a cell phone from a store. I just saw it and really wanted it, but I didn't have no money to get it so I just took it. I mean I was looking at all these kids with phones and thinking how bad I wanted one. It didn't seem fair. It was great at first after I lifted it, but then I got caught and they (the cops) told my mother and she was really angry and cried a lot. She asked me why I steal all the time and I didn't know, I just wanted to have stuff so I took it. But I kicked that. Now when that feeling comes up of wanting to steal I remind myself that I don't want to come back here (locked detention). I try to chill with friends or ride my bike instead.

Jose, thirteen years old

Jose came from a house where he was responsible for taking care of his brothers and sisters and sometimes even his mother. He didn't really know his dad and so he never asked him for help even when there was not enough money for food. Jose was out on the street at a young age hustling for money. Sometimes he did legal things like delivering groceries and sometimes he did illegal things like delivering drugs for some guys in his neighborhood. He had been arrested many times for stealing. For him it was like an addiction—when he saw something he wanted, he took it. Jose described his wanting stuff as a big hole he felt inside of him.

The feeling in his house was always sad and tense. People didn't really laugh and there was an understanding that there was never enough of anything: money, food, or love. As Jose talked about the deeper feelings behind his need to steal, like the emptiness he wanted to fill up, he began to understand his behavior more. After a while, Jose was able to stop himself before he stole and ask what was really going on inside him. The greater awareness he had over his behavior, the less he felt driven to steal. This made him feel more in control of his life and more powerful.

Passing the Blame

Another thing that entitlement may cause us to do is to blame others for the mistakes that we have made or the violence we used. If we have convinced ourselves that we were cheated, we might not hold ourselves responsible for our actions. As long as we point the finger at others for the unsafe behavior we have engaged in, we are missing the chance to take control over our lives. The more we trick ourselves into this kind of thinking, the greater the risk that we will repeat our mistakes.

We All Want to Feel Good

Let's face it, we all want to feel good. Getting things or doing things that make us feel good is part of being human. And feeling good is a good thing.

Entitlement is often our way of trying to get good feelings. Feelings of happiness, power, pleasure, belonging. And there is nothing wrong with trying to feel good, as long as you don't violate others or hurt yourself along the way. Here's a list of ways to feel good that some kids from a group came up with.

Ways to Feel Good and Stay Clean

* Chill with friends who aren't going to get you in trouble

* Get a job, because that pay check feels good

* Exercise for the "high" you get

* Listen to music

* Do art

* Go to the movies—if you've got the cash

* Read

* Meditate

* Do something positive for someone else

The Unfairness of Life

Sometimes when we feel that our life has been unfair, we feel like we don't have to play by the rules anymore. This is also part of entitlement. In a way, it's like feeling that the rules don't apply to you because you've already been cheated. And if the world or your family is going to cheat you, then you are going to cheat back. This is the kind of entitlement thinking that leads to high-risk behaviors.

But no matter how unfair life has been, **you have a choice of how you respond to all of these situations**. Let's get real, we almost never have total control over our environment. Your bike might get stolen, someone might pick a fight with you, you might get blamed for something that you didn't do. None of these things is fair and you don't have control over any of them. What you *do* have control over is how you respond to them.

Dealing with an Unfair Event

When you chose to react to negative or unfair events by taking off the gloves and fighting nasty, things could get even more unfair for you. Each time an unfair event happens to you, make sure your response is not triggered by deeper feelings about your life. For example, let's say your bike does get stolen. Do you tell yourself things like, "This kind of shit always happens to me. I have nothing and now they take my bike?" Or, "Nobody's going to rip me off anymore." Or maybe when someone disrespects you it triggers the same feelings you had when your mom put you down and made you feel bad about yourself.

These thoughts are normal. But, if you let these thoughts rule your head for a long time, you probably will use any means necessary to get back what you lost or to "right the wrong." Using violence, stealing, or damaging someone else's property could land you in jail. Now, how fair would that be?

What You Can Do to Deal with Unfair Events

1 Remind yourself over and over: The world is not out to get you. Bad stuff happens to everyone.

2 Assert Yourself—Is there a way that you can make things right without conflict or aggression? If a store clerk gives you the wrong change, you can assume she was trying to cheat you and get angry. Or you can assume she made a mistake and calmly point it out.

3 Walk away. Sometimes it isn't possible to fix things. Someone with an attitude bumps into you and doesn't say sorry. Is that fair? No. Is it worth a fight, violating probation, serving more time, or just handing your personal power over to someone because he or she has an attitude? Definitely not. If you can't fix it, walk away knowing you did the right thing.

4 See it for what it is. No matter how unfair something is, it is probably not the end of the world. Remind yourself that in a day or week, the unfair thing might not even seem like a big deal to you.

Ignore the Score

Losing your childhood to poverty, abuse, drugs, or violence is never "fair." No child deserves that. But at some point, you have to stop trying to *even the score*— for your own sense of peace. Stealing, drugging, or acting violent will not get back what you lost. It only makes you lose more. You lose your freedom, your power, and your future. Each time you act with entitlement, you cheat yourself. It's okay to say that your childhood was unfair or harsh. But if you feel personally cheated every time something unfair happens, you will experience that loss over and over again. Letting go helps you release the need to even the score.

The Gift of Resilience

If I haven't been killed yet with everything that came down on my head then nothin's gonna kill me.
                                        Jerome, Age 17

Losing your childhood because of problems in your family is tough to deal with. But no matter how tough your life was growing up, each and every one of you reading this book survived it. *If you're alive, you survived*. When a person takes a lot of hard knocks through abuse, neglect, or other trauma and is able to survive, we call them **resilient**. This means despite all of the tough and painful things that have happened to you, you continue to live and breathe and look for answers to your life. The fact that you care enough to read this book and think about your future proves that you have not given up on yourself. You know that no matter how much crap has happened in your life, there is something very real worth rescuing. Some part of you wants to heal. Because of this strength to go on and to take control of your life, you are a survivor. Strangely enough, your family gave you this gift.

Being resilient doesn't mean that you are perfect and that you will never make mistakes again. What it does mean is that you are willing to keep moving forward and to take on new challenges. It means that you are willing to deal with the past in order to figure out who you are and what you want out of life. Being resilient shows that you possess an inner strength that nobody can ever take away from you.

✋ **Stop and Think:** Take a minute and think of the strengths that you possess. Write down at least three positive qualities you possess as a result of your background. If you're having trouble seeing what good might have come from your childhood, take a look at the list some other kids came up with.

Aware of what's going on around me;
Know I can get out of a jam; Good friend;
Take care of myself and my family; Keep my cool
when I need to; Alert; Caring when someone else is in
pain; Tough; Not afraid to speak my mind

You may look at yourself and see that you are locked up and away from your friends, family, and communities. This might make you judge yourself in a negative or harsh way. By the time most kids get to the point where they are locked up, people have often been giving them the message that they are bad, useless, and stupid. You might be thinking, "Maybe I did survive, but I did a lot of dumb things too." It might be hard for you to think of yourself both as a survivor/resilient and someone who has committed violent acts or has violated the rights and safety of others. However, both of these parts of you can exist inside the same person.

Take a deep breath and repeat these words:

No matter what, the goodness and strength within me can't be destroyed.

Chapter 8

Shame and Disrespect: The Silent Killers

When I was little, my mother was always working to support us. She was a single parent so she would leave me with my grandmother. One day my older cousin and I were playing upstairs. He said that he wanted to play house and told me to lie down. Then he lied down next to me. He started to touch me and I told him to stop, but he pushed me down hard and started kissing me. I started screaming at him that I didn't want to do it. Then he climbed on top of me and started rubbing on me. I started crying and yelling until finally my sister heard me and came upstairs. She started yelling at him and pulled him off of me.

I wanted to tell my mother, but they made me promise to keep quiet so we wouldn't ruin our family. To this day no one knows but us. Every time I see him I still feel ashamed. I try not to let it get to me because I know that I didn't do anything wrong.

Ronda, 16 years old

After talking to lots of kids, we've come to believe that shame is responsible for a big percentage of the bad choices we make. Shame kicks in every time we feel really embarrassed or humiliated or when we feel worthless, damaged, destroyed, not good enough, or disgusting. Shame can be triggered when we feel dissed. Shame talks us into forgetting the power of our deeper Self. And shame fights dirty. It sneaks in the back door of your heart, mind, and soul and starts running the house. If you don't evict shame, your house (or your life) will be condemned. You cannot live at peace in a house with shame.

So why is shame such a killer? It goes right for your *heart*. Shame sends the message that you are unworthy, that you are worse than other people. If you live in the shame long enough, you will see yourself this way even though these things are completely not true. If you actually believe that you are no good because of what has happened in your past, why care about what happens in your future? That is shame talking. Shame tries to kill and destroy the core of who we are. It tries to wipe out Self. And even though that is impossible, shame is a tough contender. Unless we get control over it, shame can rule our lives.

Shame can trigger violent reactions very fast. That's why getting control of it can be a life or death situation. When we are shamed, we are often fooled by believing that destroying the person who shamed us will *unshame* us. We wrongly believe that by humiliating someone who shamed us we prove our strength, power, or worthiness. But this isn't true. Using violence to destroy shame just brings more pain to us.

Guilt and Shame: What's the Difference

Sometimes people confuse guilt and shame. Guilt can be healthy, but shame never is. Let's put it this way. Guilt is all about something you did. Shame is about who you are. Remember, *being* and *doing* are not the same thing.

Look back over your behavior for the last few months. Did you steal something, hurt someone, or lie? Well, if you did and you felt guilty, then things are working like they should. Healthy guilt makes you feel uncomfortable and tells you that something you did was wrong. Shame makes you feel that who you are is bad, no good, and not worth loving. And that is never true no matter what you did. YourSelf remains as it came into the world: always good, loving, and wonderful.

Giving Shame the Boot

To really live with peace and dignity, shame has to go. And the way to get rid of shame's poison and pollution is to use the power of Self. Each time an event or a person triggers shame in you, you can rely on Self to return you to the core of your power and dignity.

Remind YourSelf again—
No matter what, the goodness of mySelf
can't be destroyed.

The Myth of Shame— What's Wrong with Me?

Has this ever happened? The teacher asks you to read in class. You don't want to because it's hard for you, but she won't let you back out. As you read you have a hard time sounding out some of the words. Maybe someone laughs. You get stressed and make more mistakes. Now you feel stupid. You feel like everyone is looking at you. You think they finally know that you're dumb. Maybe you get so pissed off that you throw the book at a kid and tell the teacher that the kid was mouthing off to you. Deep down you feel ashamed. You feel like there is something wrong with you.

Take another example. You are in your neighborhood hanging in front of your building. A kid comes up and is looking for trouble. You're cool and don't get involved. You know he wants to mess with you. You ignore him. But then he calls your mother a drunk. You feel ashamed and like your most personal business is out there for everyone to see. All you want to do is kill him so he shuts up. Coming from a family with secrets like sexual abuse or addiction can create a lot of shame for its members. It can leave you feeling worthless or like an outcast.

Or you might feel so angry that you get totally caught up in wanting to get revenge on the people who caused you to feel shame. When these feelings are triggered, quiet the mind for yourSelf to talk. If you listen, it will assure you that you are not any of these things. Instead, you are powerful, you are a survivor, and your core is untouched by the problems of alcohol, drugs, or violence. You remain as good and whole as the day you were born. There is a strength and light to you that cannot be destroyed or broken. Even if you do not see these powerful things in yourself at first, let the Self teach you that they are there.

Stop and Think: Take a minute and think of something in your life that has always caused you shame: maybe a parent's drinking, an unplanned pregnancy, growing up poor, or having a hard time reading.

Picture this shame coming into the light. You see the shame. You are gentle with yourself. You realize that whether this thing that causes you shame was under your control or not, it did not ruin who you are. You are deeper, wiser, and more powerful than any one thing in your life.

Each time the shame is triggered, picture yourself placing it into a river and watching it float away like a small raft. You are the river, not the raft. See your shame float away with the raft. Let yourSelf remind you of how strong you are. Do this each time the shame is triggered. If you can't do it in the moment, do it later when you are calmer.

RESPECT

Disrespect and shame are like close cousins. They both are hard at work to keep you away from the power of your core Self. Because when you are disconnected from the Self, you can be played. Shame and disrespect *fool* you into thinking that destroying the person who shamed or disrespected you will make you more powerful.

The word "respect" actually means to treat someone like they are worthy. If you get respect, people are seeing the power, goodness, importance, and worth of yourSelf. If they disrespect you, they are sending the message that you don't matter or that you are worthless.

Some people confuse respect and fear. Maybe there is a guy on the street who has a reputation for being tough or bad. You might think he gets a lot of respect— but does he get respect or is he feared? Do people see who he really is or just his front? Do they like the real him or do they just not want to face his anger? Intimidation is something you force on other people. Real respect is something that people give you when they are able to see the *real you*.

Some of you might be in a locked facility right now because of "respect." When we ask kids who are locked up why they assaulted someone, they almost always say because the other person disrespected them.

Stop and Think: How do you react when you feel disrespected? Have you ever done anything violent or dangerous because you felt dissed?

The Big Question: How Respectful Are You?

It's easy to get stuck thinking about whether people are respectful to us. But have you taken a close, honest look at how respectful you are? How do you treat others who are different than you? Do you use disrespect and anger as a way to protect yourself from threatening things? Gay bashing is one of the biggest forms of disrespect out there. And it's something that a lot of kids do. And be real—it's as bad as racism and sexism or anything that disrespects and dishonors people for something they didn't chose to be.

Gay Bashing

Before you start reading, you should know that this section was written mostly for guys. If you are a girl, of course you can still read it, but we had guys in mind when we wrote it. Dealing with gay bashing is important for a few different reasons. First, gay bashing violates the rights of someone else whether you are using words or your fists. Second, being violent toward someone for any reason is a high-risk behavior and has serious consequences. Third, gay bashing has a lot to do with you trying to figure out who you are. Believe it or not. . . *Gay bashing is not about the guy you are calling "homo," "gay" or "fag"—it's about telling the world who you are.* And one thing that many guys don't want to feel is like they might be gay.

Think about your past behavior. Have you ever called someone a "faggot" or a "homo"? Refused to talk to someone that other kids called gay? Beat up or hurt someone just because they seemed gay? Some kids say that gay people deserve to be hurt because they do "disgusting" or "unnatural" things. If you have ever hurt anyone because you thought they might be gay, think deeply about what you were really feeling.

Even though they are not aware of why they are doing it, many young men strike out against gay guys because they want to make sure that no one ever thinks that they might be gay. They *want* to disrespect the guy, because it makes a statement. They think, "If I beat up a few gay guys or say cruel things to them, then people will know for sure that I'm straight." Other kids do it so that they fit in. If certain kids are treated like losers or are called gay or are made fun of, you might not want to be associated with them because you don't want people to think you're that way too. So you figure if you beat on them you'll prove how tough you are.

Many adolescents who gay bash do it because they feel very uncomfortable around someone who looks or acts homosexual. It's like just being around someone who is gay makes them feel like their own sexuality or manhood is in question. I have heard a lot of guys say, "I beat him up because he was coming on to me (whether this was true or not)." The fear is that if a gay guy came on to you, it might mean that you are gay too. So by beating up the gay guy, you think you send a message to everyone that you're not gay. You think, "Not only am I straight, but I'm tough and masculine." But if you think you are proving your manhood by victimizing someone because they seem gay, think again.

And for some kids who have been sexually abused by men, other things might be going on as well. Sometimes beating up someone who seems gay might feel like punishing or getting revenge on the man who abused you (even though the man who abused you might not be gay himself). If these feelings come up, remind yourself that violence is not the way to heal the wounds of sexual abuse.

And remember, gays don't choose to be gay any more than you chose the color of your skin or your height. Just like you didn't make a decision about whether you were straight. It's just the way you are. It is so hard to be gay in our culture. Gays are often the target of violence, discrimination, bigotry, ignorance, and hatred. Why would any one choose to deal with all of that if they didn't have to? For most people it would be a hell of a lot easier to be straight. But gays don't have a choice. It is who they are.

Let yourself really think about this stuff for a while. The next time you are about to use words or your fists against someone who is gay (or you think looks gay), think about what is really triggering you. Think about what is really scaring you into using violence. And remember the bottom line—if you feel confident about who you are, you don't need to show this kind of disrespect. *When you feel strong and connected to Self, you live and let live.*

Respect and Abusive Families

When you are respected, it is easier to believe that you are important, valuable, and have something to offer others. When people respect us, we feel like they recognize our power, dignity, and strength. Kids do not get respected when they are growing up in abusive or neglectful families. Their feelings get disrespected and sometimes their bodies get disrespected. If you are disrespected over and over, you might begin to feel ashamed of who you are.

A lot of times, young adults who are hungry for the respect they never got engage in high-risk behaviors to feel respected. They join gangs, carry weapons, act hard and tough, or sell drugs in order to get the respect of those around them. When they do this, they confuse *false power* with *real respect*. Many kids also confuse people fearing them with people respecting them. If you get people to listen to you through threats or violence, *this is not earning their respect. Fear does not equal respect no matter what they tell you or how they act toward you.*

Disrespect: It's All in the Way You See It.

Disrespect comes in a lot of packages. The disrespect

might have been something the other person said about you or your family. It could have been in a look. Maybe another guy bumped into you and refused to apologize. It might feel like the person who is disrespecting you says "You don't matter" or "You don't exist." The one thing that ties all of these things together is the fact that whatever happened, it *felt* or *seemed* disrespectful to you. To someone else, the same thing might not even be a big deal. In order to feel disrespected, you have to tell yourself and believe you were disrespected.

If you have been disrespected a lot growing up, you might be in the habit of expecting that people will naturally be disrespectful, even when they aren't.

One time one of the authors of this book was sitting in a hospital room with a young man named Bill who had been stabbed in the chest by a rival gang member. We were having a conversation about what had happened when another kid that I knew walked by the room. When the other kid saw me in there, he looked into the room and smiled at me, probably because we knew each other and he was surprised to see me there. He also looked at Bill, probably just to check out who he was. Bill took the other guy's look to be some kind of disrespect and started threatening him. Even though Bill was bandaged from his wounds and obviously in a lot of pain, he got out of bed and began walking toward this other kid as though he were going to attack him. Bill started yelling, "Oh yeah, you grillin' me? You think you're hard?" At this point the other kid told Bill that he was crazy and kept walking. When Bill and I talked about what happened, it was clear that he honestly thought the

other guy was disrespecting him by the look he gave. When I told Bill that I knew the kid and didn't think he was doing that, Bill didn't believe me. For that moment, he honestly felt "dissed" and he responded the way he always did, with aggression.

Stop and Think: Take a minute and ask yourself how often you feel disrespected by people that you don't know. Does every look from a stranger feel disrespectful? When you feel disrespected by someone you don't know, how do you respond?

Disrespect and Honor

You might feel like the only thing you have as a man or a woman is your self-respect or your honor. So maybe you believe you have to respond to everything that seems disrespectful with an attack in order to prove yourself.

In reality, no one can disrespect you unless you let yourself feel disrespected. Ever.

Some people argue that they can't let any disrespect slide because then they will seem soft and people will victimize them even more. Kids in our groups often say, "You don't know how it is on the streets. If someone disrespects me, I have to fight back." We understand that there are times that you have to defend yourself. We understand there are times when you have to look or act tough in order to take care of yourself. But to be really powerful, you have to know other ways to deal with other peoples' nonsense or you will spend your whole life fighting.

Today my impatience was triggered by an inmate who wanted me to explain how to study for the GED we are working on. He started yelling at me for not listening to his opinion about something. He was very disrespectful, I mean here I am trying to help the guy and he's giving me a hard time. I felt myself start to yell back but I became aware of my reaction and stopped. I said, "If you want me to help you, you have to stop yelling." I spoke softly and said I wasn't willing to get into a yelling match. I stayed in mySelf and he calmed down. I taught him for an hour. We talked Self to Self. Later he came back into my cell and thanked me for being so patient.

Richard, adult prisoner

Instead of letting himself feel disrespected and getting into a fight with this guy, Richard pulled back and watched what was happening. He became aware of his reaction. He chose to tap into the safety and power of his core Self instead of losing himself to a smaller, angry self. By making this choice, he let the other guy's junk go. He became calm. He was in control of himself and the situation. Each time you feel disrespected or heated, you have this choice too.

Remind yourself:

I can see this situation clearly now.

I choose to be centered, calm, and clear.

The power of decision is my own.

Dealing with Disrespect and Saving Face

Let's say that you are with some friends and somebody intentionally disrespects you by calling you a negative name or putting you down. What would you do? Is it possible to walk away from a situation like that without looking weak or soft? Can a person chose not to escalate a situation and still "save face" (not look like a jerk or a pushover)?

We know that it's hard to walk away when you feel disrespected or attacked. But the more you listen to your core or real Self, the easier it will be. You will start to understand that these acts of disrespect have nothing to do with the real you. They are a power game. Someone is trying to pull your chain and get you to react. If you lose your cool, *that person wins*. But you are not a robot. Even if your buttons get pushed, you can choose how you react.

Here's a suggestion. *Every time you feel disrespected, take a minute before you respond. Ask yourself what is really going on.*

Check out the Situation

Become an observer of what's going on. This alone helps pull you out of the drama. Every time you step back and observe your reactions or feelings, you stop being ruled by them.

Then ask yourSelf—Is the person really trying to disrespect you or did you see something that wasn't there?

Check out Your Thoughts

What are you telling yourself about what the other person did or said? The thoughts you have will determine your actions. If the person really was trying to disrespect you, are you going to get hooked into it? Are you going to let them pull you in to their game? Or are you going to see them as someone who is out of touch with their core Self—someone who is into a power act?

Quiet Your Mind

Turn off the noise in your head ("This guy can't talk to me that way and live" or "Nobody talks about my mother that way"). You can't make a good choice if you can't hear yourSelf think.

Take Control

Remind yourself again that this guy or girl does not have the power to disturb you unless you give it to him or her. Only you have the power over your thoughts and actions.

Think About It:

*In each moment I can choose to use
the power and wisdom within me.*

Chapter 9

Grief and Loss

What flashes through your mind when you hear the word "loss"? Money that fell out of your pocket? A game that you didn't win? As we go through life, losses are normal and unavoidable parts of life. Some of the losses that almost everyone goes through include breaking up with a girlfriend or boyfriend, friends moving away, and grandparents dying. It's not that these losses aren't sad or painful; it's just that they happen to almost everybody. These losses can make us stronger, wiser, and more mature. Loss has the power to deepen our appreciation of all the things we do have. And this makes life richer and deeper.

Other kinds of loss can feel much less "normal" and much more traumatic. Having a parent die when you are young and still need them to take care of you is an example. Many of you reading this book will have suffered many losses. Sometimes we suffer a serious loss, but don't even realize that we have lost something. Although we may have an emotional reaction to our loss, we might not actually make the connection between our loss and the feelings we are having.

Losses Some Kids Have to Deal With

* Having a parent abandon you or never knowing your parents

* The divorce of your parents

* Having a parent or caretaker die

* Being removed from your home and placed in foster care or adopted

* Suffering an illness that keeps you from participating in the activities that other kids are involved in— this is a loss of health

* Moving from place to place again and again and having to start at new schools and make new friends—this is a loss of stability

* Going to bad or unsafe schools where you could not get the kind of education that would prepare you for your future

* Having a parent get addicted to drugs or alcohol and losing their attention and support

* Growing up in dangerous neighborhoods where you can't safely go outside and hang out with friends—this is a loss of freedom

* Having a friend or relative die from violence in your neighborhood

* Being physically abused, sexually assaulted, or molested. This is a loss of personal integrity, meaning your right to have your personal boundaries respected. This can hurt your self-respect and esteem. You may feel like you are broken, damaged or have lost your sense of wholeness

* Being locked up in a detention center, a residential treatment center, prison, or jail. In these places you lose your ability to make many choices for yourself, like when to eat, where to go, even when to bathe

* Losing your belief or faith that you have a positive and constructive future ahead of you. Losing hope that things can be different from the way they have been in the past

* Having the world not make sense to you or having it suddenly seem unfair or uncaring

What Loss Can Make Us Feel

Grieving and feeling sadness about our losses are

140

natural and normal feelings. But there are a lot of other feelings that come with loss, too. Here is a list of feelings that one of our groups came up with:

Anger	Penalized	Need Help
Remorse	Alone	Self-Destructive
Neglected	Ashamed	Horrified
Confused	Afraid	Depressed
Sad	Down	Like Hurting Someone
Hurt	Not Loved	Like It's Unfair

Usually, the emotions you feel depend on the loss. You might be irritated that you lost your wallet. But you get over it pretty fast. You might feel upset for quite a while after a friend moves away. But some losses are bigger and more painful than others: a friend or parent dying, a parent or sibling going to jail, your house burning down. When these losses happen, we feel a very powerful emotion called *grief*.

Grief

Three years ago I was in a car crash with four other kids. I'm not sure what happened except we were drinkin' a lot and we drove off the road and the car flipped like three times. Later at the hospital the state cops came over and told me that my friend had died on the way to the hospital.

For two days I would wake up crying and throwing up. I cried myself to sleep every night.

Friends would come over to see how I was doing, but I didn't want to see no one. After a while I got really angry and was mad at everyone. People didn't want to deal with me cause I was actin' like a real b****. But inside I was feeling so scared. I felt guilty that he died and I lived. I kept thinking that maybe if I hadn't been such a screw up that this wouldn't have happened to my friend. I just wanted him to come back and have this be a really bad dream. I thought about him and the crash all the time. I couldn't get the thoughts out of my head. But mostly I felt sad that I had a future and his future was death.

It took a long time, but I'm starting to feel better now. Sometimes the sadness comes back really bad and I get depressed. I don't even feel like comin' out of my room. I can tell that people are thinkin' "Okay, get over it already." That makes me want to scream and tell them they don't know how it feels. But most of the time I feel better and better. I'm beginning to begin my life again. I think I been scared and upset for too long and I want to have a future. I need to find myself in the ruins and finish building what I been trying to build here—me.

Aisha, 18 years old

The Stages of Grief

People show grief in different ways. At the same time, there is a natural progression to grief. That means that most people's grief follows some sort of pattern. For example, you might start off refusing to believe or accept a loss that has happened in your life. Part of your mind might **deny** that it really happened. During this phase you might keep to yourself and not want to be around other people who might ask questions or want to talk about the loss you experienced.

Then you might find yourself feeling really **angry** about having lost someone or something important to you. It might seem unfair or like you are the only one going through something like this. You might be angry at God. You might be angry at the person for dying and leaving you alone.

Some kids and adults go through a stage called **bargaining** where they might try to make deals with themselves or God to bring the person back. You might find yourself saying, "I promise not to get in any more fights or steal if you just bring my father back." You might even know that this won't work, but it might feel like you're at least trying to do something about the loss.

When it finally hits home about what happened and feels real, many kids find themselves feeling really **depressed**. This is when you realize that the person is gone and will never come back. It might be difficult to think of anything else. You might feel really sad and not want to participate in the things that you used to like to do. It might seem like there is a "black cloud" hanging over your head and following you around.

Finally, however, you begin to **accept** that the person is gone or that what you lost isn't coming back. This does not mean that you will forget them or that they will lose their place of importance in your life; it just means that you accept what happened. It's like making peace with the situation. Accepting your loss gives you permission to move on with your life. Even if the loss is not someone dying, but the loss of something else, you allow yourself to become more accepting of the loss you experienced. Not everyone goes through each of the stages we just listed—and maybe you feel something else. No matter what feelings your loss brings up, accept them for what they are. The less you fight your feelings, the easier it is to eventually move beyond your loss.[2]

Releasing Our Grief and Loss

> I had two very close friends that I grew up with. They passed away from this earth when I was 17 years old. One was killed by another gang and one was killed in a car crash. It affects me to this day. I try to let it go, but it's a challenge. They are in my thoughts all the time.
>
> Victor, 18 years old

Suffering a big loss can make us feel like we're lost in a black hole. Sadness, depression, despair, not caring about anything, anger, hopelessness, and loneliness are natural feelings that we might have after a loss. Although these are normal feelings, they can take a lot of our energy. As time goes on, it's important to find ways to heal.

Unhealthy Ways to Let It Go

Sometimes when people are grieving, they find it hard to handle their emotions. Grief, sadness, and sorrow can sometimes feel overwhelming. What are some of the *destructive* or *unhealthy* ways people handle their grief?

Violence   When you push your real feelings down, they do a real number on you. Instead of feeling the pain, you might look for someone to pick on or abuse. You dump your pain on others.

Drugs or alcohol   This might feel like a solution to getting away from the pain, but it only allows you to escape for a short time and brings on a lot of other problems.

Masks   Sometimes the loss is so painful that it feels safer to wear a mask as a way to avoid the pain. This is not a long-term solution.

Turn sadness on ourselves in destructive ways.   Some kids hurt so much from loss that they cut themselves or give themselves painful and dangerous tattoos to feel like they are reducing the emotional pain they have.

Hurting Animals   Animals are living creatures who feel pain as much as humans. If you take out your pain on animals, find a healthier way to let your hurt and sadness go.

Other High-Risk Behaviors   High-risk sex, stealing, or other behaviors that put you in danger might let you forget about your grief or suffering for a while, but they carry consequences that can make you feel worse in the long run.

Healthy Ways to Let It Go

There are ways to grieve that do not place you or others at risk, but still release the pain.

Talking Talking about what you are feeling with someone you trust is a powerful way to release pain and sadness. The connection we feel from communicating can bring us strength and support.

Crying   Anyone who has ever had a really good cry can tell you how much it helps to release the pain and sadness that gets carried around in your body and mind. It's like having a storm sweep through you, leaving clear air in its trail. But letting yourself cry can be hard for people to do, especially for young men. Growing up, you got the message that crying means you are weak or a sissy. If it is hard for you to cry in front of people, find some privacy and give yourself permission to cry there.

Remembering   If the loss was the death of someone close to you, it can help to remember things about that person with friends. Keeping his or her spirit alive through memory can bring us a sense of peace and calm.

Art or Music   These things can help us relax and release pent-up emotions. Also, some people find that they can remember a person or a place they have lost through art or music.

Visiting   Returning to the place where the person was buried or their ashes were released allows us to stay connected to the person even though they are no longer physically present in out lives.

Rituals or Celebrations   Keeping certain rituals or celebrations that allow you to remember the person in a positive way. Maybe you light a candle for the person on their birthday or go to their favorite place once a year.

Grieving Takes Time

Like all acts of healing, grieving takes time. One day you might feel good and think that the pain is behind you. But the next day you find yourself lost in darkness or sadness again. This can be tough and scary, because you thought the despair and pain were over only to have them come back. You might ask yourself, "Will it ever end?"

You might have heard the expression that "time heals all pain." And there is some truth to that. Be gentle with yourself. Try not to tell yourself that you should "be over it by now." With time and a commitment to healing the wounds of loss, you will move beyond it. And every loss we survive adds to our strength and resilience.

Chapter 10

Our Friends, Our Choice

Families are not the only influences that shape our lives and how we choose to live them. This is especially true as we get older and spend more time with friends, girlfriends, and boyfriends. The main difference between our families and friends is simple: we don't chose our families, but we can chose our friends.

Are Friends Safe to Make?

When we work with young men who have been arrested and placed in detention centers and residential treatment centers, we often ask them about their friendships. Most of the kids we talk to say that they don't have friends. When we ask them about the people that they hang out with, they tell us that these are their "associates." At first we didn't really get it.

But over time it became clear to us. These guys had been hurt, snaked, disappointed, and let down so many times that their hearts had become closed in order to protect themselves. It all came down to trust. For some, the issue was not wanting to be hurt emotionally. For others, trust was a matter of survival. I sometimes watched the guys hanging out together. Anybody could see that many of them felt a genuine warmth toward each other. They wanted the goods that friendship offers: companionship, protection, someone to listen to you, and someone who really cares. But all the time, one eye was watching their backs.

Trust

It is hard to trust friends, but if trust is put on me then I feel I have collateral and they trust me and I trust them. But the thing is, trust can always come back and bite you in the ass.

Phillip, 18 years old

To Trust or Not to Trust?—That's the Real Question

We don't just get our beliefs about whether it is safe to trust our families, friends, and girlfriends/boyfriends overnight. Babies don't come into the world suspicious of everyone, prepared to be disappointed, watching their backs. We build these beliefs over time. We learn from the way our families and friends treat us. If people are there for us, we usually believe the world is trustworthy. Of course most of us have been lied to, cheated on, and let down at least once. Unfortunately, it is part of life. However, if we are disappointed or treated unfairly time and time again, we believe that we can't trust anyone but ourselves.

Nobody's Fool

There is an old saying, "Trick me once, shame on you. Trick me twice, shame on me." This basically means that you should learn to be suspicious if someone cheats or hurts you so that it doesn't happen again. By being on your guard all the time and expecting that everyone has bad intentions, you can protect yourself from getting hurt or looking stupid. Unfortunately, if you choose to live your life this way, you will give up a lot. You give up the chance for love, intimacy, and caring. You make a choice that being alone (or building up walls around yourself) is better or safer than building a group of people you can trust.

As you get older, it is possible to create a different kind of "family" built from friends. But in order to surround ourselves with loving and caring people we need to do two things. We need to learn how to trust and be trustworthy. And we need to choose the kinds of people who can be trusted.

Your Trust History

Stop and Think: Think about the level of trust you give to people in your life. Think about your family and friends, both past and present. Is there anyone you trust in your life now? How about in the past? How did that person get your trust? Did he or she have to earn it or did you just give it to them? What would you do if that person broke your trust? Could they ever get it back? Do you think that you are someone that others can trust? Is there anyone in your life who trusts you?

Showing the Real You

Letting someone get really close can sometimes freak us out because we think they'll see us for who we are. We think, "If they really knew me, there's no way they'd ever come back. I lose my temper sometimes. I'm a bad dancer. I'm too bossy." But who are you *really?*

Underneath these small parts of your personality (bossy, grumpy, bad dancer) is the core Self. And the true Self of *everyone* is wise, strong, good, and lovable. Next time you feel that no one could love you if they knew you, remind yourself of *who you really are*.

Do You Deserve My Trust?—A Section for Young Women

Let's be clear. *Not everyone deserves our trust.* You've all been around long enough to know that some people are not mature enough to treat us with the respect, dignity, and caring that we deserve. The better you become at seeing this, the easier it will be to trust. If you are in an abusive relationship now, take a close, hard look at why you are staying.

I stayed in an abusive relationship because I loved him and because I had a kid with him. I got out because it got to the point where I started thinking with my head instead of my heart. He came from a bad home and he never had no one to show him how to love. I kept thinking I could be the person to open his heart— to show him how to really be with someone. Plus, every time I said that I was leaving he would say how he couldn't live without me and how he would kill himself. I felt guilty about that. I think he wanted to change, but he wasn't ready. Yeah, he was my son's father, but I got to make the right choice for me and my baby.

Another reason I stayed was because my father was never around and I didn't want my kid to feel like that. But I asked myself what kind of

*message was I sending my son. I don't want
my kid to grow up watching his father beat
on me. I moved out, took my stuff, and took
my son. He still comes around to harass me
or to beg me to go back with him, but I
don't think that a man should ever put his
hand on me especially if he says he loves me.
So the thought of being with him again won't
cross my mind. I do think I still love him, but
I can't put myself back in that type of situation again.*

Rosemary, 19 years old

No matter what, there is never a good reason to stay in an abusive relationship. Even if you have a child together—especially if you have a child together. That doesn't mean that guys who abuse can't change—they can. But it takes a lot of hard work on his part (like counseling or support groups for batterers)—not just promises.

Many young women have spent a lifetime watching their mothers get involved over and over with men who did not deserve their trust. You saw the pain and the hurt that these men brought into the lives of the people that you loved. Perhaps each time she found someone new, she would believe that things were different this time only to be hurt, cheated on, used, lied to, rejected, and disappointed again. You might even have found yourself getting involved with men who did the same types of things. Maybe you believed that this is just how man-woman relationships work.

My mom always got involved with men who used her. It was like she walked around with a sign on her back tellin' men to take her money, mess up her house, and cheat on her. No matter what, she would always take them back if they showed her some love. In a way I'm like that, too. I always get with guys I know are kinda bad boys. That's just the kind I seem to be attracted to. But I know how to take care of myself. I don't let them walk over me like my mom did. I give as good as I get.

Tonya, 18 years old

Unconditional love doesn't depend on our performance. It is always there. For those of us who never knew this kind of acceptance, we are used to taking the kind of "love" that comes with strings. We might find ourselves settling for "love" that places us at risk, uses us, abuses us, victimizes us, and threatens to leave us if we don't meet its demands.

Ask yourself honestly whether you are addicted to the thrill of the make-up break-up cycle. He does you wrong, you break up, it feels bad, he begs for you to come back, you get together, it feels good. And the cycle continues over and over. *The cycle of high-risk love is the same as any other high-risk behavior.* You become hooked on the drama. Although this cycle of ups and downs might feel familiar and predictable to you, it usually ends with someone getting hurt.

These drama relationships are imposters of real love. In healthy love, the core Self of each person is respected and honored. To connect with the deeper Self of someone else, it helps to be connected with your core Self first.

Setting Boundaries with Boyfriends, Girlfriends, and "Just Friends"

When I got pregnant, my boyfriend's attitude started to change and he started talking to me like I didn't matter anymore. He wouldn't take me anywhere with him, and he left me in the laundry mat by myself to wash his clothes. I would text him and he wouldn't call me back until five hours later. He wouldn't put any attention on me and he expected me to stay at home all day. He expected me to cook food for him no matter what time of day it was. He used to embarrass me outside and yell at me in front of everyone and just act really dumb.

I really felt like I didn't want to be with him anymore. I regretted getting pregnant with him. Then one day I just couldn't take the pressure anymore. I got mad and just went off on him and told him how I felt. I told him that the relationship was going nowhere, that I didn't know what I felt for him, that he wasn't the person I fell in love with, that I was not sure if I wanted to be with him. I told him he had two weeks to change his attitude and his actions. And if he didn't get it together that I was not going to be with him because he was not there for me.

Ever since then, he comes home by one o'clock. When he sees me sleeping he makes his own food. He's looking out for me and the baby now and he knows what he has to do. He's there for me physically and mentally and that makes me feel good. If I hadn't drawn the line, I think we would not be together now.

Jamie, 18 years old

Sometimes we find ourselves in relationships that we think are fine—at first. Then it becomes clear that we are being abused, disrespected, walked on, cheated, hurt, or played. We then have to make a decision—Do I stay or do I go? And if I stay, what are my limits? Jamie's story is a good example of someone setting boundaries. That means she took a hard look at her relationship and decided what she would put up with and what she wouldn't. She realized that she deserved more than what she was getting. She decided that if her boyfriend didn't change, she would have to leave. Although a move like Jamie's takes guts, each of you reading this book has the *power to set boundaries* for yourself. In Jaime's case, her boyfriend was willing to change. But setting boundaries with someone doesn't mean that they will do what you want. It just means that you are not willing to stay in a relationship where you are not getting what you need or deserve. Even if your mother or father couldn't set limits with their partners—you can.

Trusting People Who Can Be Trusted

Let's say we've scoped the person out long enough to know he or she is trustworthy. So what's the problem? Why can't we really trust? Even letting someone who seems emotionally safe get to know us can feel like high-risk behavior. And it is. But becoming trusting is a risk that leads to self-growth, not self-destruction. Getting to know someone on a deeper level, allowing them to learn about who you are, and sharing your feelings can feel very threatening to a lot of people. We get scared and say to ourselves, "What if I get too attached? They might leave and cause me pain." These are risks we take when we become close or intimate with people. However, these are risks or challenges that can lead to positive and loving relationships. By staying closed, we miss an opportunity to feel a strong connection to someone. And it is through these connections that we learn about ourselves, our strengths, and the power of our true nature. By staying closed to others, we stay closed to ourselves.

The Power of Choice

Part of learning about ourselves and gaining greater power over our lives is actively choosing the kinds of peers that won't drag us down. We have to develop a kind of *trust radar* and use it. Who can we trust? Who can we depend on? We need to be assertive when choosing the types of people we are willing to let into our lives. That means that we aren't willing to hook up with someone we know is a threat to us.

Is Trouble Knocking?

There is a big difference between not knowing that a peer is going to be trouble and knowing that he or she is bad news, but going along with him anyway. Do you find yourself making friends with people that get you into bad situations? Do your friends seem cool but then talk you into doing high-risk things? Maybe sharpening your *trust radar* is a good idea.

Exercise: Imagine that you're a cop sitting in your cruiser by the side of the highway. A cop knows exactly how fast a person is driving by pointing a radar at the car coming toward him. Let's say that your trust radar works sort of the same way. When a new person comes along and wants to be friends with you, point the trust radar at him or her to find out how trustworthy he or she is. What does the trust radar need to tell you about the person? What questions should the trust radar ask? Here's a list that one group came up with. Did they get them all?

→ **What do I know about this person?**

→ **What kind of reputation do they have?**

→ Who else do they hang out with?

→ What does she or he do for fun?

→ Is this someone I can trust in my house?

→ Is this person going to steal from me?

→ Is he or she positive in the community?

→ Is she or he in a gang?

→ How does this person handle conflict?

→ When I'm around him/her, do I act like myself or am I putting on a front?

→ Does he or she pressure me to do things that I don't feel comfortable about?

→ What does my instinct tell me about this person?

If you ask yourself these questions and your trust radar doesn't tell you whether this person is a positive or negative peer, take it slowly. Don't rush into a relationship if your gut says that there might be trouble.

Stop and Think: Take a moment and think back on the kinds of friends that you have had throughout your life. Were they a good influence on you or did they lead you to participate in high-risk and dangerous behavior? Looking back at your past friendships, do you see yourself as a leader or follower? Do you go along with the ideas of your friends even if they are dangerous or could lead you into trouble?

Peer Pressure

I was 13 years old and I was hanging with an older crew of guys maybe 16 or 17 years old. We were walking downtown and the guy who was kind of the leader told me to snatch a gold chain from this old lady waiting for the bus. Truth be told I didn't want to do it. But he kept saying it and I felt like I had to. I went up to this lady and asked her if the clock in front of us was right. When she looked up I snatched the chain and ran. I gave the chain to the guys and they sold it on the street for like twenty bucks or something. I got caught about two hours later. I didn't rat the other guys out so I did two months in lock up—alone.

Isaiah, 16 years old

What are some of the reasons that kids give in to peer pressure? Read through this list and ask yourself which ones you have experienced in the past.

1. To "save face." This means to keep yourself from being embarrassed or looking weak. You might have a reputation as tough or cool that you want to keep or you might want others to start thinking of you that way. Basically, you don't want to be teased or humiliated by the people pressuring you.

2. To be accepted by a group of people and fit in—want to be down

3. To prove something to yourself or others

4. Sometimes the people pressuring you to do something threaten you if you don't do it.

5. You don't want to be the one to "ruin the fun" or "bust up a party"

6. Sometimes things just start to happen and you have a hard time finding the right time to back out

Look at that last one on the list. You might find that peer pressure sort of sneaks up on you and that you get carried away in the moment. For example, some kids find themselves involved in a high-risk behavior that gets more and more out of control and, rather than asserting themselves and backing out, they follow it through.

If this happens to you, you need to find good "*escape hatches.*" Some kids say lie if you have to. Say your parents grounded you and you can't go out. Say you're sick. Say whatever you have to in order to stay out of a high-risk situation. This means that you need to listen to your inner voice when it first starts to tell you that things are getting too wild or out of control. **When in doubt, get out.**

Gangs

Being in a gang seems like fun when you're young. You get caught up in all this negative shit like doing drugs, drinking, fighting, getting locked up. But then when you get older you might be sick of it. I mean you might want to do something positive with your life and then it's too late. When you try to change, your enemies remember you. And they come looking for you for revenge. But because you left the gang, your homies don't have your back anymore. You got no one to back you up and then you end up on the run to stay away from people. So that's it, man, once you in, you made your bed.

George, 18 years old

We once asked a group of guys how many of them were in a gang or knew someone in a gang. One guy looked at us and said, "What exactly do you mean when you say *gang*?" And he was right. The word "gang" has a lot of different meanings. When we say *gang*, we mean belonging to a group involved in high-risk activities—any group that moves you away from the real power of your core Self toward the false power of the gang.

In this section, we talk about the emotional factors that cause people to join gangs. If you are already in a gang, we're not judging you. We are not telling you what you should or shouldn't do. We're hoping to help you get greater Self-awareness about what pulled you in and whether you want to stay.

Gangs—Do They Really Protect You?

Learning the World Is Unsafe

Nobody is born violent. We learn violence. And the reason that most kids learn to use their fists or weapons is to protect themselves. If you are beat up going to school every day or threatened with a knife or a gun, the first thing you might have done is tell a teacher or your parents. But maybe these adults were unable or just refused to protect you. Maybe the adults in your family or community were afraid of being the victim of violence.

Stop and Think: Think back to a time when you needed to be helped or protected by an adult. As clearly as you can, remember the situation. Did the adult step in and help you or did they ignore your call for help? How did you feel about the way things worked out? Did it leave you feeling safe and protected or weak and defenseless?

Looking for Safety

Human nature makes us want to be safe so that we can survive. Nobody wants to feel like they are going to be gunned down or jumped each time they go to school or walk to the store. For many kids it is better to look and act like you are angry, dangerous, and ready to go off on someone than to feel like you might get jumped or scammed. But even if you look like the toughest, hardest guy or girl, that might not be enough to protect you. Even if you are willing to fight over and over again, you might still get jumped or threatened. So where do kids turn when they feel like they need protection but they can't get it from their families, teachers, or adult neighbors? Many kids turn to gangs.

The Myth of Protection

I first joined a gang because I was raised in a bad neighborhood. Almost everyone on my block was in a gang. And if you didn't join, some other gang would start to pick on you and mess with you and you couldn't be safe or just left alone. Being in a gang made me think I'd be the kind of guy who got a lot of respect. But I didn't really. The only thing I got was to learn to talk a lot of shit and goin' through bad things like getting locked up. When you're in a gang, everyone is kinda scared of you and everyone kinda hates you. You feel like you always gotta watch your back, even though you joined so you would be protected.

Lawrence, 17 years old

The problem is that gangs offer a *myth* of protection. That means that it promises one thing and gives you another. Many kids who join gangs are shocked when they figure out the level of violence and danger inside a gang. They feel they opened themselves up to even greater levels of violence than they had been exposed to before they joined. This makes them grow deeper into the role of violence and further from their true Self. They often feel pushed to do things that go against their judgment and their sense of right and wrong. It is the ultimate form of peer pressure.

Although a gang might protect you in certain situations, it places you and your family in danger. All of a sudden you are the target of people you don't even know. Conflicts from before you joined can put your life at risk. *So where's the safety in that?*

Gangs and Power

I spent most of my life bein' like overlooked by everyone or forgot. I come from one of the worst neighborhoods in the Bronx and the schools and parks were run down and dangerous. The teachers never listened to what I had to say. I didn't get in a lot of trouble, so in a way, I was just like invisible. My parents had a lot of problems and didn't really notice what I did that much. Once I got pulled over by store security because they thought I stole something even though I didn't. My parents don't speak too much English and they couldn't really help me out. I was just sitting there for a long time feelin' totally powerless and like anything could happen to me.

Jose, 17 years old

Some kids deal with these feelings of powerlessness by joining gangs. Being part of a gang can give you a sense that you have some weight and that you can control things around you. You think a whole group of people is there to back you up, to fight for you, to give you the power you didn't have before. You think kids will treat you differently if they know you are in a gang. Maybe by victimizing others, you feel like you can get control over all the times when you felt like the victim.

Many kids who are in gangs find that the power they experience comes with a big price tag. The biggest thing they talk about is the control they give up over what they do and the choices they have. If you are in a gang and they tell you to rob a store, steal a car, or jump a kid, how much of a choice do you have? Would you say, "I'm gonna pass on this one, folks"? Do you have as much personal freedom to make the kinds of choices that are best for you? Belonging to a gang can give you the physical power of many people, but it also means that you lose a great deal of control over your choices and your future. If you think that gangs make decisions with your best interest in mind, you are seriously fooling yourself.

The Power of a Gun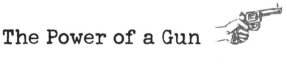

My friend was killed last year in a gang-related shoot-out. He was shot three times in the face and two times in the chest. I felt like I had lost my brother. During the funeral *when I saw his face in my mind, I hoped he would go to a better place than the one here on earth. He was a very nice person. Every night I go to sleep I can picture the place where he was killed. His death changed my life. I don't want the same thing happening to me.*

Darren, 17 years old

One of the big things that has changed in many neighborhoods, especially those in big cities, over the past twenty or so years is the number of guns that have found their way into the community. It used to be that when kids had a problem, they would fight it out with their fists or in the worst case with a knife.

This chapter is not a place for us to argue how dangerous carrying a gun is. Just by looking around you can see that people who carry guns are much more likely to die from one than those who don't carry. It is an extremely high-risk behavior. Just like joining a gang, the power you get from a gun opens you up to a new level of risk and potential for violence.

A Place to Belong

When I was around thirteen, I felt like my life was just a play on stage or an experiment that GOD was doing. I got involved in a gang

*because I wanted to feel a sense of belonging.
I wanted to feel like people cared about me.
But a gang to me now is something that I wish
I didn't join. I learned that a gang can make
you feel comfortable and happy for a while, but
it will not keep you safe forever. It will not
give you a future if that's what you want.*

Darnell, 16 years old

For people who never got a sense of love and belonging from their own families, the pull to join a gang can be very powerful. If you spent your whole life feeling like nobody really cared about you, a gang can feel like the answer. It is human nature to want to be surrounded by people who accept us. Many kids report feeling closer to their gang members than they do to their own family. It's like they say, you can't choose your family, but you can choose your friends (or your gang).

*I got involved with a gang because of the lack
of love and care in my family. I grew up in a
single-parent family. My mom was always out
working and trying to make ends meet. Trying to
fulfill the American dream. She tried so hard
that she forgot to be there when I needed her
the most. So I went out to the street
searchin' for love and somewhere to belong. It
didn't feel like being in a gang, it felt like a*

family. But it was the kind of family that could get you killed real fast.

David, 19 years old

Is This Who I Really Am?

One of the "jobs" of being a teenager or young adult is figuring out who you are and how you fit into the world. For some kids, joining a gang can be like getting an *instant identity*. That means that before you joined a gang you maybe weren't quite sure who you really were and maybe you weren't sure if other people knew. After you join a gang, however, you are a Blood or a Crip or a Latin King or a _____. Now they see you as tough, backed up by a crew of other people, someone to be feared and, you think, respected. Maybe in your neighborhood people look at you in a whole new way. And this might feel good to you, for a while.

But once you decide to join a gang, your identity comes under a powerful force. You are no longer free to pick and choose how to conduct yourself. Instead, you are told. It's like surrendering your true Self for a false self. And while the power you get (or take) from others might feel good in the short run, what you sacrifice is much greater.

Gangs and Role Models

For those of you locked up for selling drugs, you know that there is a "gang mentality" that goes along with the business. Not every gang sells drugs and not all drug trading involves a gang, but the two things are not so different.

There is always a pecking order or rank system in the drug trade, with one or two guys at the top and everyone else falling in beneath them. Many kids who have joined gangs or started selling drugs have talked about how these older guys seemed like father figures to them. These guys often seem powerful, have a lot of cash on them, drive nice cars, and have big reputations. They often give new kids extra attention or make them feel like there is something unique or special about them. This is especially true for guys who are recruiting you to hustle for them. They draw you in with cash and special treatment and make you feel that you are going to be just like them, running the show some day.

Father Figures

Being singled out for special attention can be a powerful trip for kids who never knew their own fathers well or at all. Even if the guy is a cold-blooded killer, we often mistake their attention for "love." Wanting to be loved like a son does not make you weak...it shows that you are human. In fact, wanting to be loved is healthy and natural. The problem comes when you go looking for love in the wrong places.

These older guys might be the first people to give you money or allow you to do something that seems important. They might seem to treat you with respect and trust you with their money and their drugs. These guys might seem like everything a man is supposed to be: smart, tough, makes a lot of money, and powerful. You might find yourself wanting to become like them.

It doesn't take long to figure out the down side of these relationships. Screwing up one time can mean your life. Kids start to realize that they are being used by the dealer to make money and that these guys care only about their business—not about the kids they use to sell their drugs. Many of you might be locked up because you took the fall for an adult.

In the video series *Homeboys: Life and Death in the Hood*[3], we hear from young men who all were either members of the Bloods or the Crips. One guy on the tape talked about how he started selling drugs when he was twelve because he looked up to the older guys who were running the business. He talked about never knowing his own father, but wishing that his dad was like these guys who gave him money and promised to protect him. After he got really involved in the drug trading, the big money that they had given him in the beginning stopped coming and it became clear that they were using him. They didn't care if he lived or died as long as he sold the crack they gave him and returned every day with their money.

Stop and Think: If you never got a chance to know your father or if you knew him only briefly, there may be a lot of things you want to say to him. And even if he's not around, you can still tell him how you feel. Imagine for a minute that your dad is standing in front of you. He asks you in a genuine way what it was like to grow up without a dad. What would you tell him? What did it feel like not to know your dad? How did you feel about yourself? How did you or do you feel about him? Does it affect the kind of parent you are or want to be?

Now, imagine that it is your dad's turn to talk. What would you like to hear from him?

The Real Role Models

Sometimes I feel like my life's been shut down— even when I know that people around me care about me. Not knowing my father makes me feel like I don't have a clear vision of myself at all. It's like a hole inside me. I wake up and look in the mirror and I don't know who I am. How I'm gonna figure that out is a mystery to me.

Michael, 16 years old

Figuring out the kind of man or woman you want to be is a tough job. But the job is even tougher if you didn't really know your mom or dad. You might ask yourself, "How's a real man/woman supposed to act?" You know in your gut that a man's not supposed to run out on his family, but what is he supposed to do? This is where finding good role models can help us figure out where we want to go.

You might not have grown up with your father as the role model of what a man is supposed to act like, but there are definitely men around you who might be a model to you. The same goes for women. Maybe your mom didn't live a life that you want, but you are free to look for other women to be role models. Finding people we admire and want to be like can help guide us and give us goals. But finding role models requires you to make some decisions about who you are. If the people you admire and want to be like are sending the message that drugging, robbing, carrying weapons, and using people are the way to get power and respect, there's a problem.

✋ **Stop and Think:** Take a minute and make a list of the people you consider to be your role models. They can be people in the neighborhood, athletes, family members, or anyone who you respect and admire. What is it about them that you admire? Their lifestyle? The way they handle themselves? The things they have achieved? Their outlook on life? How caring they are?

If you look at the role models you have chosen and found that they include people who promote violence or high-risk lifestyles that place you or others in danger, take some time to think about this. What is it that makes these people attractive? Do they seem to carry a lot of respect, authority, or power? Have they made a lot of money, and if so, what does that mean to you? What is it that they represent to you?

The Last Word

Take a look at who your friends are—who you've signed on with. If you see that these people are pulling you in the wrong direction—do something. It might feel hard to pull out when the car starts rolling down the hill, but it becomes much tougher as it picks up speed. Remember—you have the last word on who you hang with—use it.

Chapter 11

Offending Behavior:
Taking Responsibility – Taking Control

Chances are if you are reading this book, you did something that got you in trouble. But what about afterwards? Did you step up and own your behavior? Can you admit what your real role was or did you try to pass the blame? The point of this chapter is not to attack you or make you feel bad about yourself. What we want to do is show you that you have the power to make choices at every step of a situation. Even after you make a mistake, you have the power to regain control over your life by accepting responsibility for your actions.

Taking responsibility for your offenses or the hurt you caused others is simply a choice that you make. It's not magic. Taking responsibility is simply a decision. And it's not always easy. **But either you stand up or you don't.**

Before continuing in this chapter, take a minute to do a check of your body. Do the words "taking responsibility" trigger any feelings, thoughts, or physical reactions? Do these words make you feel defensive or like you need to protect yourself? If they do, try taking a few deep breaths and relaxing.

The Way of the Street—Deny, Deny, Deny

Looking at your behavior honestly and accepting responsibility for your actions can be tough. We often believe that admitting our mistakes means we are weak. We become programmed to think that saying we were wrong means "backing down." In fact, nothing could be farther from the truth. Owning your responsibility requires far more strength than running from a situation. You have to be more of a man or woman to accept responsibility. **And being a real man or woman requires you to own your actions.** If you want the monkey off your back, you have to come clean.

Stop and Think: Ask yourself honestly how you deal with making a mistake. Do you automatically try to get out of trouble by denying and lying? Has this worked for you in the past? Do you usually see yourself as "set up" by other people? Do you take

177

responsibility for your actions and choices? Do you fool yourself about your involvement and responsibility by always making excuses?

Giving Guilt the Slip

You might be stuck in a pattern of thinking that goes like this. "So what if I stole from that store. They aren't gonna miss that CD. They make so much money that this CD is nothing to them. It's not like I stole it from a person. I bet they never even notice it's missing. They rip people off by charging way too much for these things anyway."

Sound familiar? This is the kind of talk a person does in their mind to try and convince themselves that the mistake they made isn't a big deal. It's called rationalization. And it's a way that we try and talk ourselves out of feeling guilty. It's a way of making something wrong seem right. This kind of thinking is extremely dangerous because it allows us to not feel guilty for doing something that is wrong.

So What Is Guilt?

I don't feel guilty for no one. Ain't nobody feel guilty 'bout me.

Troy, 16 years old

When we talk about guilt, we don't mean the legal guilt like when you go to court. We mean the kind of guilt you feel (or should feel) when you've done something wrong. Believe it or not, guilt is a healthy feeling.

178

Guilt can be our alarm to stop doing something wrong. Feeling healthy guilt helps us make good choices and allows us to control our behavior. Guilt can guide us to behaviors that are honest, respectful, and just. But sometimes we become numb to our healthy guilt.

Becoming numb to our healthy guilt is extremely dangerous. It sets you up on a dangerous cliff with no net. Having no guilt lets you stop taking responsibility for your behavior even in the privacy of your own mind. You become deaf to the voice of your conscience (inner voice) that tells you when you have done something wrong. The longer you are deaf to guilt, the harder it becomes to take responsibility for your actions.

The Three A Words You Need to Know

For some of you, even those convicted of an offense, you may never have admitted to yourself what you did. Many kids who have been arrested and "punished" in some way for their negative behavior become so defensive that a *real* conversation about their feelings of guilt is not possible. They become masters of getting away with things, pulling cons, and denying their involvement. Cornell West, a professor at Harvard, once said that for many kids, "The 11th commandment is 'Thou shall not get caught.'" If this sounds familiar to you, for the rest of this chapter try and take a vacation from those thoughts until you finish reading.

When you commit an offense, you violate the rights of others and give away your power and respect. Restoring balance and healing from that mistake is a process. *It is possible to serve your entire sentence and never really close the chapter on your offense.* So how do you really move beyond your mistake? We believe the first three steps in dealing with your offense are what we call the three A words.

The Three **A** Words

Acknowledging what your *real* role was in the offense

Accepting responsibility for your behavior

Apologizing to your victim or the people hurt by your actions

Step 1. Being Honest With Yourself—Acknowledging

It wasn't my fault, man. It was the weed.
Derek, 15 years old

The first step of taking control over your behavior is to *acknowledge* what you did. Sounds like a big word, but it's simple. It just means to be *truthful* about your role in the offense. To do this you need to be completely honest about the way you operate. To acknowledge your role, just answer this question....

Did you do it?

Look into your heart. Ask yourself…
What was your real role?

Step 2. Moving Beyond—Accepting Responsibility
If you accept responsibility, then you can look yourself

180

in the mirror and say...

I did something wrong.

If you have to use with the word BUT, you are not accepting responsibility.

If you say, "Yeah, I did it, BUT he deserved it..."

Or "Yeah, I beat her up, BUT she started it..."

Or "Yeah, I stole it, BUT I needed it..."

Or "Yeah, I was there, BUT I was just the lookout..."

YOU ARE NOT ACCEPTING RESPONSIBILITY
Go Back to step 1.

In order to move beyond your offense history you have to be totally honest with yourself about what you have done and the price you and others have had to pay— emotionally, physically, and spiritually. This can be difficult because thinking about our negative actions can bring up really painful feelings. It might call up what others have said about us in the past: "We knew he'd end up in jail" or "That girl is rotten to the bone." If you admit your responsibility, you might ask yourself what kind of a person would do a thing like that.

These negative feelings can be so powerful that we will do almost anything to avoid experiencing them. If we convince ourselves we didn't do something wrong or hurtful (when we did), we can avoid feeling the uncomfortable feelings that go along with knowing that we did hurt someone. Some of you might be spending a lot of energy and time trying to convince yourself that you are not responsible for your mistakes. But unless you come to terms with these feelings, they become like a weight that will drag you down.

> For real, it feels great to come clean and be honest. You don't want to be keepin' something inside you that you're all worried about—havin' a lot of nightmares, bad dreams, and everything else. When you release it to a person or to a group of people that you trust it feels good. Your body feels free and you don't care about it no more. It's out of your mind and it's out of your heart.
>
> Arnold, 16 years old

Growing up (emotionally and spiritually) requires us to take responsibility. If we don't take responsibility, we stay stuck. Taking responsibility allows us to grow up—to grow wiser and stronger.

Unhealthy Guilt

Sometimes healthy guilt turns into unhealthy guilt. How do you know the difference? Well, healthy guilt is a signal that something you did is wrong. It is our conscience kicking in and keeping us straight. Unhealthy guilt is beating yourself up over and over again for something that happened in the past. It's like driving your car into mud and getting stuck there. Every time you hit the gas, you sink deeper and deeper until you can't move.

Feeling unhealthy guilt is like turning against yourself. It creates a lot of tension and negative energy that you need to release. Many times that tension gets released by getting involved in a high-risk or offending activity. That brings on more trouble and more unhealthy guilt. If you're not on top of it, unhealthy guilt turns into shame. And we know that shame does nothing but eat away at your self-esteem, your power, and your ability to deal with things the right way.

So how do you get rid of unhealthy guilt? Well, the first step is to come clean about the negative acts that made you feel guilty in the first place **(acknowledge)**. The next step is to **accept responsibility** for those actions and to **apologize** even if you can't talk to the victim. We'll talk more about apology later. The next step is to **forgive yourself** for what you did. Only through forgiveness can you see your mistakes for what they were: attempts to get the power, acceptance, and love you felt you were missing. We'll talk more about apology and forgiveness later.

 Stop and Think:

Your Offense History—Without beating yourself up, try and remember all of the offending behavior you have been involved in. The big offenses might come to mind first. But try and think of the small things like jumping turnstiles and stealing candy bars. How old were you the first time you committed an offense? What is the most serious thing you've done?

Holding on to Offending—
What I Get out of It

No matter where you're at in terms of your legal or criminal record, take some time to look at the types of negative power trips you may use in your daily life. These behaviors could include intimidating, lying, cheating, threatening, controlling others, and using violence. And most important, you need to stop for a minute and realize *why you use these behaviors*.

On some level, pushing your weight around and using negative power tactics has gotten you *what you want at least some of the time*. If you're jealous and insecure about your girlfriend hanging out with other men, you might have beat her up to scare her. If you want to send the message to another kid that you are not to be messed with, you try to intimidate her. If you want a bike but you don't have the money for it, you take one. And if you get what you want each time you pull a negative power act, then why stop?

Fortunately, you're smart enough to know that getting things this way has some major drawbacks. You realize that if you continue to lead this type of lifestyle, you'll always be looking over your shoulder, just waiting to get busted. Part of you, even if it's only the quiet voice of Self, sees the problem with getting things through negative power acts. Most people who get things this way end up in prison, ashamed, dead, in trouble with their families, and watching their backs.

The Impact of Crime and Abuse— Seeing Your Victim

As long as you can't see the victim, it's like it never happened.

Joshua, 17 years old

Real honesty means seeing *all* of what we have done. Only then can we learn from our past and move on to the emotional freedom that the truth will give us. The act of taking responsibility connects us with Self—even if we don't think about it like that.

Part of being entirely honest about your offense is looking at how your behavior impacted your victim. Being the victim of abuse, violence, or theft can emotionally damage a person for years. Victims of violent crimes may have trouble going to work, socializing with friends, or sleeping in their own homes. They may relive the crime over and over, never trusting that they will be safe again.

In the period right after a crime, most victims are overwhelmed with feelings of confusion, helplessness, terror, and vulnerability. These feelings are usually followed with feelings of anger, guilt, suspicion, depression, and self-doubt. There are questions that might haunt a victim for a lifetime: Why me? Is the offender coming back? What could I have done to stop it from happening? Victims often feel that God has left them to fend for themselves.

Being in the Victim's Shoes

I remember being real young and comin' into my house and seein' the place tore up. It was like the third or fourth time we were robbed, but this time it looked like a tornado ripped through it. My shit was everywhere. They took the TV and the VCR. They even took some of my sister's toys. What the hell did they want toys for? My mother was cryin' and runnin' around. My sister and brother were cryin' too. When I started robbin' people, I never thought about how it would make them feel. I just shut my mind off to that and thought about how much we'd get from them. I didn't think of them as real people in a way.

Justin, 16 years old

Sometimes people who have been victimized end up victimizing others. By being the one who assaults, steals, or vandalizes, people feel they take on a powerful role and get rid of the weaker, vulnerable feelings they had as a victim. But victimizing is false power. It makes you a victim over and over again because each time we hurt or violate others, we dim the light of our true Self. We betray ourselves. We hurt our families. And it sometimes results in our freedom being handed over to others.

Pebbles in the Pond

When I robbed those two guys I made them victims. I made their families victims 'cuz of how they was scared about their kid. I made my mom a victim because she was upset and angry, plus she had to find the money for my bail when she didn't have no money. The people in the 'hood was victims, too, 'cause they wasn't letting their kids out because they was scared it might happen to them.

Oonnell, 17 years old

Ever thrown a rock into water? The rock enters the water in one place and makes a splash. Then ripples start moving out from the center and the circle becomes larger and larger. This is called the ripple effect. The same idea applies to any type of offense that you commit against someone.

Think about someone who is the victim of a violent crime. Let's say that a man is stabbed and robbed on his way to the store. He spends several weeks in the hospital recovering. Every night he wakes up from terrifying nightmares as the attack gets played out over and over again in his mind. Now he is afraid to leave the house. He misses so much work that he is fired. His family has a hard time paying their bills and his wife has to go out and get a job. The kids are scared and confused because their family seems to be falling apart. He becomes very depressed. Other people in the community start to feel scared to go out at night because they worry about getting attacked.

Although you might think that an act of violence only affects the victim, that's not true. It affects everybody who is in that person's life.

![hand icon] **Stop and Think:** Take a minute and think back on the most serious offense you committed or an act that affected a person in a negative way. Who else besides the victim suffered because of your actions? What did the mother, father, aunts, uncles, sisters, brothers, friends, grandparents, children, or wife or husband of your victim feel? Truly acknowledging our role and accepting responsibility means that we understand all of the people who were affected by our action, not just the primary victim.

✋ **Stop and Think:** Look at the chart. It shows how crime is like a bicycle wheel with the spokes moving out from the center. Your offense is in the middle, with people close to the victim being touched by what you did. For each of the people listed in the chart, think about the consequences that they experienced because of your actions.

Nonviolent Crimes — A Bigger Deal Than You Might Think

Some of you reading this chapter on victims might be saying to yourself, "Hey that's not me. I'm just in this place for selling drugs. My crime didn't have any victim. They wanted drugs and all I did was to sell the stuff to them." Think again.

We once asked the following question to a group of kids in a group: "Do nonviolent crimes like selling drugs or stealing from a large company have victims." We were surprised at how quickly they said *YES*. We then asked them to explain what they meant and this is basically what they said: *Selling hard drugs always hurts someone because they mess that person up and the person using them is an addict who is suffering because of what you gave them. If you are selling drugs to kids you are doing the same as killing them because you might as well be dead than to be a junkie.*

You might try to rationalize your behavior and say, "Well, if I didn't sell it to them, someone else would have." The bottom line is that someone else didn't supply them. You did. Seeing this is part of standing up and accepting responsibility for your actions.

I was selling crack before I got here. There was this one lady who was always comin' around me buyin'. She was a real crack head—always wearing nasty clothes with some crazy ass hair. Anyway- I was doing this girl that I really liked. This shorty was hot and she was in my crib one day. I heard the door knock and when I looked outside, it was this crack head lady. When I opened the door my shorty said, "What's my mom doing here." And I was like, "Oh shit, that's messed up, I'm selling crack to her mother." I felt real bad. I felt real guilty about that.

Jamel, 17 years old

Stealing from a company also means there are victims. Even if you think your actions are small and don't matter, they do. You might not be able to see the face of your victim, but he or she is there. Telling yourself that the company has lots of money and that they will not miss the money is just more rationalizing. No matter how faceless, powerful, or rich your victim is, the fact is still the same. Every act of victimization, *no matter how invisible it might seem, is on you.* It weakens your backbone, it weakens your integrity. Getting this is part of accepting responsibility for your actions.

190

Step 2. Apologizing

Me and my friend were friends since we were six years old. But no more. When I turned 15 years old, I slept with my friend's man. I knew she liked him, but I didn't care. I kept up the relationship behind her back. She always suspected it, but I lied and never told her the truth. After a while she found out about it from other people. But it should have been me to come clean - her own best friend! I always thought I could just take what I wanted in life. But now I realize that it's not like that. It hurts me that I lost a friend like that for a guy I didn't even love. I think it would have been better to be honest with her. Sometimes I wish she would talk to me so that I could apologize to her. I feel bad that I hurt her. Once I wrote her a letter saying how I was sorry. I didn't mail it, but just talking out what was in my heart made me feel better.

Shanila, 16 years old

Once you have taken the brave steps of acknowledging to yourself what you have done to hurt others, and after you have truly accepted responsibility for those acts (admitting you did something wrong), you're almost ready for the next step. The next step is to apologize to the person you have hurt. You might not be able to speak to your victim directly. And contact with the person you violated might not even be a good idea. However, in order to move toward your own healing and empowerment, you must truly apologize for the harm you caused your victim (even if you can't say it directly to them).

Many things stop us from apologizing. If you watch little kids on the playground, you can see how early it starts. One kid might push another one or grab a toy away from him. His mother might tell him to say sorry, but he won't. He looks at the ground, gets an angry look on his face, and says that he didn't do anything wrong. If you have never really apologized before, the first few times you try it might feel strange to you. But just like other things in this book, new things only feel strange for a little while.

Some kids refuse to apologize because they are *angry at their victim for telling on them or turning them in.* Some of them even have said that they plan to get revenge on their victim when they get out. This is big time rationalizing. By making the victim wrong, you can feel okay about your offense. You can even fool yourself into thinking that the victim *victimized you* by turning you in. It's an eye for an eye thinking and it will leave you blind.

Stop and Think: What do you think about apologizing? Do you see it as something that makes you stronger or weaker? Do you see it as giving power to someone else or as making you a stand-up person? Have you ever seen anyone truly apologize for something he or she did? Do people in your family apologize to one another when they make mistakes?

Is It Sincere?

We've all heard someone offer an insincere apology. That means they say sorry, but we know it's just a line. Maybe they look at you and say, "Sorry, my bad," but you know they don't really mean it. You can't fake an apology and have it do the work of really freeing you. To truly apologize, you need to consider the pain of your victim.

What usually keeps us from apologizing is not wanting to take responsibility for what we've done. It can be very hard for us to really accept some of the things we have done. We do not want to accept responsibility because we are ashamed. But once we really believe that the Self is good, kind, and lovable *no matter what we have done*, we can see for real that our actions are separate from ourSelves. Taking responsibility for our negative behaviors does not make you a bad person. It makes you a strong one.

Apologizing without Expectations

I was gonna say sorry, but he was all hatin' on me, so forget it. I ain't apologizin'.

Gerald, 16 years old

Apologizing sets you free, but only if it is done from the heart and without any *expectations*. You do it because it's right. You do it to release the burden. But don't assume that your apology will be accepted. If you do, you are setting yourself up to get an attitude if your apology is refused. Even if the other person is not ready to forgive, it has nothing to do with the steps you need to take for your own healing. You can still apologize and you can still forgive yourself. The people you hurt may not be ready to let go of their anger. They may be too frightened or wounded to let go of their anger. Allow them to be where they are. Respect their right to feel the way they do. It's okay to want them to forgive you, but we can never force a person to do this. Don't get caught up in needing their forgiveness in order to let go of unhealthy guilt.

Ways to Apologize

Apologizing can take many forms. It can be a conversation with the person you hurt—face to face or by phone. It can also be done through a letter. Although many kids find writing difficult or unpleasant to do, it lets you really plan what you want to say.

Writing

Writing a letter of apology can be a very powerful way to express your feelings about what you have done. Even if you throw the letter away or never send it, putting your feelings and thoughts into words on paper can help you move down the path of healing.

When Tony Hicks was 14 years old he shot and killed an 18-year-old pizza delivery man named Tariq Khamisa. Tony had a lot of problems in school and at home. His mother and father had abandoned him and he was being raised by his grandfather. Soon, Tony started hanging out with a gang in San Diego. They got together and smoked marijuana and drank beer. When they ran out of money or beer, they stole what they wanted. One night they decided that they would order two pizzas, distract the delivery guy, snatch the pizzas, and take off. When they began their mission, they brought along the 9mm gun that Tony had stolen from his grandfather's house. Instead of conning the delivery guy and running off with the food, Tony pulled the gun and threatened him to hand over the pizzas or else. When Tariq said "No," and started to drive away, Tony shot and killed him. Prior to his conviction, this is what Tony said about the murder:

Q-Tip (another gang member) starts shoutin' at me, "Bust him, Bone, bust him. So I did. I pulled the trigger. The nine kicks hard, the window broke, and the pizza man yelled. Blood was comin' out of him. I knew he was hurt bad. . . It was all cool. I didn't think I was gonna get in trouble. Only homeboys saw what happened and they weren't gonna snitch.

When questioned by the police, Tony told them that the pizza man had been stupid for not giving up the pizzas. He had been killed for $27.24 worth of food.

Tariq had been very close to his father, a man named Azim. Although Azim was devastated by his son's death, he did not feel hatred in his heart for Tony. As he saw it, two lives had been destroyed because of this senseless act of violence: his son's and the shooter's. Azim did not spend his time hating Tony and wanting him to be punished. Instead, he saw Tony for the angry and confused boy he was. Tariq's father forgave him for taking his son's life. He started a foundation to help children and teens find non-violent solutions to problems and worked closely with Tony's grandfather making the project happen. Through Azim's forgiveness Tony was able to accept responsibility for killing Tariq. Eventually, Tony felt deep empathy for the father whose son he killed. This is the letter he wrote to the judge before he was sentenced to 25 years to life in prison.

Good morning, Judge.

On January 21, 1995, I shot and killed Tariq Khamisa, a person I didn't even know and who didn't do anything wrong to me. On April 11, 1996, I pled guilty to first-degree murder because I am guilty. I wanted to save the Khamisa family and my family from further pain.

From my grandfather, I have learned about the Khamisa family and their only son Tariq. I have learned about the love they have for him. Through my grandfather and Mr. Reynolds, they have tried to explain to me the compassion the Khamisa family has for me.

I have had a lot of problems in my life. Over the last year, while in Juvenile Hall, I have thought about my problems. I wish I didn't have the type of life I had. I wish I had a relationship with my father. I think about the warmth my grandfather gave me. I wonder why I didn't listen and learn. Now, I wish I would have listened to my grandfather.

At night, when I'm alone, I cry and beg God to let me out of here. I promise Him that I will be a better person—I won't mess up. When I see my mom, I want to hold her as tight as I can, and beg her, 'Take me out of jail!'

However, I don't want to use my problems as an excuse for my actions. I think I would have gone to jail sometime but I honestly don't think getting busted for a robbery or something like that would have changed me. I was too mad at everyone. my mom, my dad, my grandfather. When I first came to the Hall I was mad at the O.A. and the people at the Hall for keeping me here. Now, I'm just scared and mad at myself.

I'm alone at Juvenile Hall. Even though the people at the Hall are pretty cool, I'm still alone. I often think about the night I shot Tariq, especially when I'm alone in my cell. When it's dark and quiet, I wonder what it's like to die. I wonder why I'm still alive. Sometimes when I roll over in bed and I lay next to the cold wall, I feel as far away from everything as possible. I wonder if that's what dying feels like.

I still don't know why I shot Tariq. I didn't really want to hurt him or anyone else. I'm sorry. I'm sorry for killing Tariq and hurting his family. I'm sorry for the pain that I caused for Tariq's father, Mr. Khamisa. I pray to God every day that Mr. Khamisa will forgive me for what I have done, and for as long as I live I will continue to pray to God to give him the strength to deal with his loss.

My grandfather promised me that he will be Mr. Khamisa's friend and help him in any way that he can for the rest of his life. I am very sorry for what I have done. Thank you for giving me the chance to speak.[4]

Make It Right

Apologizing is something you've got to do to really stand up and take responsibility for your offense or mistake. But it isn't always the final step. If it is possible, you need to repair the damage you did by paying back. When you can – make it right. This might happen in a lot of different ways. If you stole money from someone, return it. If you spent the money, then work to get the money to repay the person. If you stole an item that can't be replaced, find out how much it costs and give the person that amount of money. If you started a rumor about someone and it hurt them or their reputation, you need to fix it by coming straight. Sometimes we won't see our victim again, but we know that we have wronged someone. If this is the case for you, try repairing the damage by doing something kind for someone else. It won't undo the damage you did to your victim, but it will help someone else. And that's a powerful thing.

*　*　*

Many people believe that the things you just read about in this chapter (*admitting* or *acknowledging* your offense, *accepting responsibility* for your offense, *apologizing,* and *repairing the damage* in whatever way possible) can leave you with a great feeling of freedom. It is like a weight has been lifted from you.

Now, find a place where you feel comfortable. Take three deep breaths and feel your body relaxing. Picture yourself carrying a large box on your back. It is heavy and you feel smashed down from having it on your body for so long. You were instructed that to remove the box, you must admit your wrongdoing, accept responsibility, apologize, and pay back in whatever way you can. You have done these things. It was difficult, but you succeeded. Now imagine the box being lifted from your back. As the weight comes off, you feel your body rise up. You feel taller and stronger. You walk with a new feeling of dignity and respect. Your eyes, which have looked hollow and dead, become alive. There is a power shining from them.

Chapter 12

Self-Forgiveness

It seemed like I'd been a screwup my whole life. And I mean stupid stuff all the time. I would skip school, drink, smoke weed, come in at all hours of the morning. And my mother would be cryin' all the time and screamin' how she couldn't take it anymore. I always saw the trouble I got into as my problem - not hers. Then the last time I got locked up, my mother came to see me and she looked bad. I could tell that I had really disappointed her and hurt her. I could see in her eyes that she was scared for what was happening to me and where I was going to end up.

I started feeling really bad about what I put her through. All of a sudden it hit me what a bad son I was. I never thought about how she was feeling or what she was going through because of my actions. Then I looked back and saw all the problems I had caused different people. I felt like shit about it.

I worked hard to put things right with my family. I told my mother how bad I felt about what she went through on account of me. I took a hard look at myself and tried to take responsibility for the things I done. After some time I started to forgive myself. I realized that feelin' bad all the time about it was getting me nowhere. It felt like a relief to ease up on myself. When I started forgiving myself I stopped feeling like a dark cloud was always right on top of me.

Ricky, 17 years old

The Heart of Healing

When most kids first hear the words "self-forgiveness" they think, "Forgive myself for what? I didn't even do anything." Or maybe even, "Yeah, I stole it, but it wasn't my fault." If this is where you're at, you're not ready for the next step. Go back to the three A's in chapter 11.

If you've really accepted responsibility, what now? The next step is the heart of what it takes to heal yourself from the past. This step is called *self-forgiveness.*

Way down inside, you might think that you can't forgive yourself. You might think, "If they only knew some of the shit I've done, they wouldn't be talking about self-forgiveness to me." Actually, there is *nothing* that you cannot be forgiven for—*no matter what you have done*.

What Self-Forgiveness Is Not

Before we get into what self-forgiveness is, let's talk about what it is *not*.

Self-forgiveness is *not* convincing yourself that an offense you committed was not an offense. It is *not* getting out of taking responsibility for your actions.

Self-forgiveness does *not* mean you quit paying attention to the feelings or situations that trigger your high-risk behavior. Paying extremely close attention to these clues will help stop you from re-offending. Preventing yourself from re-offending is *your* responsibility.

Self-forgiveness is *not* avoiding feeling guilty after you have done something wrong. Owning up to your mistakes is part of growing up. If you really hurt someone—even killed someone—you will regret your actions for a lifetime if you are in touch with your heart. But as time goes on Self-forgiveness lets you learn from your mistakes, then lets the pain soften. The way you feel about yourself isn't ruled by your past actions forever.

With Self-forgiveness, you are not forgiving the acts you committed, you are forgiving yourself.

202

What Self-Forgiveness Is

Self-forgiveness has two steps. First is looking at your mistakes and being willing to learn from them (doing the 3 As). Second, is *really getting* that you are a good person—no matter what you've done or what's been done to you.

Getting the Job Done

So, how do you forgive yourself?

First, remember, you're not a bad person—*you never were.* You were a confused person who made mistakes or did bad things. Take full responsibility. Learn from what you've done. But don't get stuck beating yourself up for those mistakes. Remember that those actions are not who you are.

Some kids feel like they have two sides to them. The *negative side* that does the things they shouldn't do and the *good side* that usually stays out of trouble. Only by really looking at your negative acts with some gentleness can you heal. Beating yourself up will not work. Drugging or sexing to avoid the pain will not work. Only self-forgiveness will allow you to heal your feelings of guilt and shame.

Give Yourself a Break

How often do you beat yourself up or put yourself down? You think judging or nagging yourself will make you better or stronger. It does the opposite. By always judging, *we set ourselves up.* . . busting on our looks, our bodies, how much money we have, how smart we are. When we compare ourselves to others we usually feel like we come up short. Give yourself a break. Let go of the criticism. Stop bad mouthing yourself long enough to see that you're really okay—No matter what you wear, who is on your arm, what your ride is, or what others have said about you in the past.

Seeing It Through

All forgiveness means that you are finishing business and putting something to rest. You can use your imagination to help close the chapter of your negative actions. Stop for a few minutes a day. Imagine being with the person you hurt or violated. Imagine sincerely apologizing and asking for forgiveness. Try to forgive yourself, even if the person you hurt can't forgive you. See if you can find it in your heart to wish them well even if they don't wish you the same. Just asking for forgiveness and offering it to yourself is an act of true strength.

Remind YourSelf:

No matter what I did, the goodness of mySelf can't be destroyed.

Chapter 13

Forgiving Others

Have you ever thought, "I'd never forgive that person after what they've done"? As if by forgiving the person you're doing them a favor. In truth, forgiving someone is a favor you do for yourself. Would you consider letting go of your grudges? Not for anyone else's sake— just for your own!

Two years ago my baby's mother did something that I will never forget. For a long time all we did is scream and yell at each. other. Then she threw me and the baby out of the apartment. I felt like I wanted to kill her. I was so angry that every time I saw her or heard her name I would go crazy. I was dangerous *and I didn't have control over my feelings. I knew that I had to change something because I didn't want my son to see me like that. I felt like my anger was choking me. Forgiveness helped me a lot. When I forgave her, I felt like I let go of something. I forgave her to get a better life for me and my kid.*

Jake, 18 years old

Like in Jake's story, the biggest reason to forgive is to *free yourself.* If you don't forgive, it is like you're handcuffed to the person you're angry at. Even though you don't mean to, you drag them around wherever you go. It's like you're pulling a heavy load around with you all the time. Do they really deserve that much of your time and energy? Maybe it's time to put some of that energy toward taking care of yourself…thinking about what might make YOU happy instead of putting so much of your attention on the past. Being stuck in the past sucks a lot of energy out of the present and can close off any positive pictures of the future…if you let it.

Forgiveness frees you so that you are not battling the ghosts of your past every day. Instead of making us soft or weak, forgiveness gives us back our power. As long as we spend our time hating and resenting, we are handing our power over to that person.

Getting Clear on What Forgiveness Is NOT

Let's be clear. When we talk about forgiveness, we DO NOT MEAN that it is okay that harmful experiences happened to you. We DO NOT MEAN that the people who hurt you should not be held responsible for what they did. And most importantly, if you are still in an abusive situation, the most important thing for you to do is get help. That might mean telling someone who can keep you safe, calling a hot line, or simply getting away. If you don't know who to call, look at pages 252-255 in this book for telephone numbers or ask a counselor. Before you begin forgiving, you must be SAFE.

Let's say you are a young woman involved in a relationship with a guy who verbally and physically abuses you. A lot of the time he is sweet. He buys you things, makes you feel beautiful, and seems to treat you like an adult. But when he's stressed out or drugging, he snaps. Once he hit you so hard that you flew halfway across the room. After he hits you, he always says that he's sorry. You make excuses for him and tell your friends that he didn't mean it. Maybe you think it's the last time he'll do it because that is what he tells you. You're afraid to leave him. When he asks if you forgive him, you say you do. **THIS IS NOT WHAT WE MEAN WHEN WE TALK ABOUT FORGIVENESS**.

Staying in the relationship and making excuses for someone who's abusive so that you don't have to break up is not forgiveness. Forgiveness is not accepting or allowing harmful behavior to happen to you. Forgiveness is not letting yourself be a victim. It is not letting people walk all over you.

It never means sacrificing your safety so that abusive situations stay the way they are.

Forgiveness does not mean that you have to let the

person you forgave back into your life. It doesn't mean that you want to hang out with them even if they have changed their behavior. You can forgive an old friend who betrayed you or sold you out, but you never have to hang with that person again—unless you want to.

Forgiveness is not forgetting. When you forgive, you don't forget. Instead, the painful and angry feelings that come up when you see that person or think about them start to fade away. Or if the angry and hurtful feelings do come up, they don't last as long.

What Forgiveness IS

Imagine you have a cousin about your age. When you were growing up, he acted like a bully. He'd take your things without asking, lie to your family about you, and push you around. Over the years, it got so that you couldn't stand the sight of him. Every time you saw him, he set you off. In fact, just the mention of his name would make you angry. After spending time with him during the weekend, you'd find yourself thinking of him all week long—thinking about how much he pissed you off.

Here's where forgiveness comes in. You can choose to see only what's on the surface of this kid. You can choose to see his negative behavior as him just being a jerk. Or you can use forgiveness. Forgiveness is a choice to see a bigger picture. By forgiving you see a kid who used sneaky games and low-down tactics to get attention and feel big. A confused guy who never figured out a better way to fit in.

By forgiving, you're not saying what he did is okay.

You're not forgiving the acts, you're forgiving the person. If you let yourself stay angry at him—you become an actor in his drama. Poof, your power is gone.

But if you see the lost guy beneath his act, you can step out of his drama. Forgiving him frees you because you are no longer hooked into the old anger and grudges. By making the choice to forgive, you see a person's immaturity or power tripping for what it is— an expression of how disconnected they are from their core or true self.

So What's in It for Me ?

When you forgive, it lets you step back from the situation and see everything more clearly. Forgiveness gives you three major things:

> 1) You feel less anger, so your head doesn't get so messed with.

> 2) Because you feel less anger, you won't be as likely to strike out against people.

> 3) Because forgiveness lets you see a situation more clearly, you keep control over yourself. *You keep hold of your power.*

Forgiveness is not a one-time event. You may genuinely see and forgive in one moment. Ten minutes later you might be angry again. At each of these moments of anger, you have the power to see the situation more clearly.

Where to Start

It is hard to get into the right frame of mind to forgive if you are very angry. The first steps of forgiveness begin with dealing with your anger. If you need to, re-read chapter 3 on anger.

There may be certain people that you are not ready to forgive right now. The wounds might be too fresh or deep. We're not telling you that you *should* forgive. If you are not ready or willing to forgive right now, that's perfectly okay. But even if you're not ready to forgive the big things, **FOR YOUR SAKE** try forgiving people you've got little battles or grudges with. Then you be the judge of whether you feel better and more in control.

Forgiving Our Parents

I learned in life that everyone is human and everyone makes mistakes. The hurt and anger my mom put me through by not showing up for me made me realize that she could not teach me what she does not know. I know no one ever showed her love or good feelings or how to be a good mother. She taught me something big. That is forgiving someone when they can only do what they are capable of. It makes me feel less angry and makes my life easier without being so mad. I feel more humble towards others in life.

Marshall, 18 years old

Our parents can often be the most difficult people in our lives to forgive. They are often the first people in our lives to hurt us. And what's worse, they hurt us when we are totally dependent on them. Years of disappointment and resentment may have been building up. Forgiving your parents is not something you decide to do one time and then it's all over. Forgiving your parents is a decision you make to understand their behavior on a deeper level. It's about seeing them as real people who make mistakes and messed-up choices because of their own confusion, fear, and insecurity. It is about freeing yourself, not them, from these negative emotions.

As you think about the idea of forgiving your parents, you might be saying to yourself, "I have a right to be angry after what they did to me." And you are absolutely right. You do have the right to be angry. Maybe your anger isn't in the past, because your parents at the moment are not supporting you, caring for you, or showing their love. It's hard to work on forgiving your parents if you are still really angry at them. If your anger is too strong at the moment to move beyond it, just be gentle with yourself.

When Parents Don't Act Like the Parents We Want

Although your parents may be older than you in years, inside they might be like wounded children. They might be thirty or forty years old on the outside, but scared six-year-olds on the inside. Many of your parents did not have safe and happy childhoods themselves. They did not get loved the way kids should. Parents often can't do a good job providing for their kids if they are stuck in their own pain and confusion. Forgiveness helps us see that our parents' faults and weaknesses are not about us. Their problems are about them. Forgiveness lets us take our parents anger, unavailability, and abandonment less personally.

Expectations: The Pain of Not Getting What You Wanted

My mother was never really there for me. She had a lot of problems with drugs my whole life so mostly I grew up with my grandmother. I saw my mom sometimes and she was part of my life, but she wasn't the one who helped me with my problems or gave me comfort when I was upset. When I found out I was pregnant, I thought my mother would change. I thought now that she was going to be a grandmother herself, she would be there for me and the baby. The whole nine months I convinced myself that she would turn around when the baby was born. Well, the baby was born and guess who was there for me in the delivery room and helpin' to take care of the baby when we came home from the hospital? Yeah, my gram, not my mother. I was really upset for a while. I cried a lot—askin' myself why she didn't want to be *there for us. I really believed that she would change. I guess I should've known better. I mean, she was never there for me before. It would have saved me a lot of pain. I'd still like more from her, but I'm getting better at accepting her for who she is.*

Sharon, 17 years old

Have you ever had a picture in your mind of how something would be and then found yourself really let down because your expectations were not met? It happens to everyone. Sometimes, having an attitude of "We'll see what happens," can lead to less disappointment.

One sure way to set yourself up to be mad at your parents all the time is to have unrealistic expectations of how they should act. When we say expectations, we mean things like expecting your dad to show up for your basketball game when you know he probably won't. Or expecting your mother to get excited over a passing grade in school (or some other success) when you know she has a hard time being supportive. Of course it would be great if your parents or grandparents did these things. But if you know that they probably won't, be realistic about what you expect from them. Expecting more than they can give will only bring you more pain and disappointment. Part of growing up and letting go of our anger is seeing our parents' (and others') limits.

This might seem like harsh advice, but think of the alternatives. You can be realistic about your parents, let go of the expectations, and be less hurt when they act the way you thought they would. Or you can have big expectations, be totally disappointed when they don't deliver, and have a lot of anger afterwards.

Remember, forgiving your parents or other people who have caused you pain or disappointment doesn't usually happen overnight. It can take time and work to forgive. You may feel like you finally forgive someone, then, bang! A memory comes up that triggers your anger again. At these times, don't judge yourself. Be patient. With people who we have a long history of being angry at, forgiveness is something we may have to choose over and over again. But each time you choose forgiveness, you let go of the weight you've been dragging around. And you're free.

Meditation: It's Not What You Think

The idea of meditating might sound totally weird to you at first. But it's one of the most powerful ways to reduce stress and create inner peace. It's so powerful that the Chicago Bulls and Los Angeles Lakers have used it for years to get their players to become more centered, focused, and aware. Meditating makes the players sharper and better. In fact, the man who teaches the Lakers and Bulls meditation learned to meditate from one of the authors of this book.

Meditation has many forms, but a core part of all of them is focusing one's attention and awareness.

Meditating: Why Bother?

Your mind is a high-powered thought machine. It is constantly filling your head with opinions, judgments, questions, memories, fantasies, and every other kind of thought possible. When left alone, the mind is rarely quiet. *Meditation is a way to find peace in the very center of your thoughts and emotions.*

Ever feel something (like anger or sadness) so powerfully that you got swallowed up by it? Stress can be like that. When you're stressed, it's as if your head is in a cloud and you can't see the calm, clear sky that is always there above. Meditation lets you get back to that clear sky *whenever you want.*

Think about it. How good a player would Michael Jordan have been if he ran around the court like a crazy man just chasing the ball? Not very effective, right? If you act on every feeling or thought you have, it's just like chasing the ball around the court. Wouldn't it be better to watch what's going on? Then you can see the play, make a clear choice, and control the game. Meditation helps you do exactly that.

Losing IMPULSIVITY and Gaining CONTROL

How many of you have been told by adults that you are impulsive? Impulsive means that you *act without really thinking.* Some of you might be reading this book in a detention center because you committed an offense by acting without thinking of the consequences. Maybe you got caught in the heat of the moment. We have spoken to many kids after they had committed various offenses. Time after time they would say, "It was so stupid, I don't even know what I was thinking."

Meditation is a powerful tool that helps you become less impulsive. It gives you space in your head to think. In fact, the more you meditate, the more likely you are to think before you act. It helps you resist being pulled into things that you're likely to regret later.

The most important attitude to have about meditating *is a willingness to try*. Someone once said that meditating is like lifting weights. Lifting weights makes you stronger even if you don't believe it "works." You show up at the gym, start off slowly (5, 10, or 20 pound weights), use the proper techniques, and soon you are stronger than when you started. The same is true for meditation. You start off slowly (5 or 10 minutes), use the techniques, and soon you feel like a calmer, less angry, more centered person. Even if you don't believe that it works, you'll soon see that it does.

How to Meditate

Simple Directions

1) Sit down
2) Be quiet
3) Pay attention to your breathing.
Feel your belly rising and falling with each breath.

The Extended Play

1. Find a comfortable sitting position where your back is straight. Let your body be balanced and at ease. Place your hands comfortably on your lap or knees. Close your eyes. If you aren't comfortable closing your eyes, you can chose a place nearby and focus your vision in a relaxed way.

2. Bring your attention to your breathing. At first you can focus on your belly rising and falling. Notice the changing sensations in your body as you breathe in and out. Just feel your breath. Don't try to control it. Breathe naturally. Sometimes your breathing may be deep, sometimes it may be shallow. Your "job" is to simply be aware of your breathing and the changing sensations in your body as the air goes in and out.

3. Your mind will naturally wander away from your breathing again and again. When you realize that your mind has drifted, just notice it with a "no big deal attitude" and return your attention to your breathing again.

4. After focusing on the belly for a while, you can expand your awareness beyond the belly. As you breath in and out, become aware of the changing sensations throughout your body. Again, remember, it's normal for your mind to sneak off into other thoughts. Just gently bring it back.

5. Do this everyday. Shoot for at least fifteen or twenty minutes everyday. If possible, choose a regular time. It makes it easier to remember to do it. **Even if you feel weird doing it at first, go through the motions anyway.**

Meditation works.

Meditating Throughout the Day

In addition to the more formal meditation practice when you set special time aside to meditate, you can practice in a less formal way throughout your day. Meditation can be done while walking, lifting weights, eating, exercising, and riding the bus. Basically, it can happen any time throughout the day.

To meditate in this way, become aware of your breathing from time to time throughout your day. Do this for a few breaths. Bring your full attention to the present moment. Become aware of whatever is going on.

Common Questions and Comments about Meditation

Here are some questions kids have asked about meditation.

Is it okay to lie down to meditate, rather than sitting up?

During the practice of meditation, it is okay to lie down, but it's better to sit up. Find a comfortable position with your back straight but relaxed. You can sit on the floor, in a chair, or on a pillow with your legs crossed. Sitting helps you be awake and alert. And these are the states of mind that you are trying to bring to your meditation. The mind is naturally more likely to drift if you are lying down. Also, you are more likely to fall asleep.

 I'm trying, but it's hard to stay focused.

When you start meditating you realize very quickly that the mind has a mind of its own. The wandering mind is just part of the process of meditation. Your attention will naturally move away from the breath many times. Within moments, your mind may start to doubt, criticize, or question what you are doing. The practice of meditation is noticing that the mind has wandered and coming back to the breath without judging—time and time again.

When your mind wanders, just treat it with a "no big deal " attitude. It's just the mind wandering. Then bring your attention back to the breath again. Come back to the present moment. Rather than thinking about staying focused for the next five minutes, be more realistic—try and stay focused until the next breath. See if you can be aware from the beginning of the breath coming in all the way to the end of the breath going out. Feel the rising movement. Then feel the falling movement. When your mind wanders, gently bring your attention back to the breath again. Know that if your mind wanders a hundred or a thousand times in an hour, the meditation still has great value. As you do this, the mind becomes steadier and more balanced. Your job is not to judge how you are doing. Your job is just to do it.

Sometimes I feel peaceful when I meditate, some times I feel uptight. Am I doing it right?

The practice of awareness meditation is simple, but not easy. Before you know it, you may find yourself having lots of experiences. You may feel peaceful and calm while meditating or you may feel restless and uptight. Your mind may be quiet and still or flooded with many thoughts. You might find it easy one day to focus on your breathing and impossible the next day. Whatever your experience of the meditation is today, it is likely to be different tomorrow. As long as you follow the guidelines suggested, and you give it your honest best, you are doing the meditation correctly.

Sometimes it's really difficult to meditate when I'm feeling angry or frustrated. It's hard to be there with myself. I'd rather get up and walk away.

It's hard to sit with our pain and misery. It can

feel overwhelming, like that's all there is and that's all there will ever be. It takes a lot of courage to not run away from these feelings. But the more you can sit with these difficult feelings, the more you find you can handle them.

Soon after I start meditating, I seem to fall asleep or get tired.

Try meditating with your eyes open or even standing up. Sometimes practical solutions like putting cold water on your face can help.

How can you meditate when there is so much noise around?

The way to deal with noise while you're meditating is the same way you deal with anything else that comes up during meditation. Don't judge it or get caught up in it. Just notice it. Simply notice "sound." Don't label the sounds as "voice," or "banging," or "music." Simply notice sound as sound. In meditation, everything that arises is given equal attention and value. Rather than judging one sound as pleasant and another sound as unpleasant, simply notice sounds coming and going around you. Also, notice the sound is "outside" of you. Then notice, by contrast, how quiet it is "inside" of you.

I keep finding excuses not to meditate. When I meditate I know it helps me, but it's hard to find the time.

We have to *make* the time to meditate. If we don't, we will almost always find ourselves doing something else. If it's the end of the day and you're too tired to sit for fifteen minutes, try meditating for a few minutes instead. You'll be amazed at how much you will gain from even such a short time meditating.

It is very helpful to meditate around the same time each day so that it becomes a regular part of your schedule. Meditating in the morning can set a good mood for the rest of the day. Problems will still come up, but you are more likely to be ready to deal with them in a more relaxed frame of mind.

And each time you meditate, you get in touch with the power of Self.

Chapter 15

Spirituality

I saw guys who had been using drugs and who were cold-blooded jerks find God—and you see a miracle. You see them completely change. You see them start to care about others. You think if there was hope for that person, if that person could change, then there's hope for me, and you want what they have. You begin to believe and to know that there's a greater power directing things because you see that power reveal itself. For me, it's not about reading the Bible or going to church. It's about a connection. It's about the way you live your life. It's like there's a bigger plan and your life fits into it.

Arnie, adult prisoner

Finding a Connection

We worked with a 17-year-old named John for a few years. For most of his life he'd been getting into trouble for stealing, truancy, and fighting. He'd gotten in so much trouble that his mom had pretty much given up on him. She stopped going to his court dates and didn't know where he was half the time. But John's big problems started when he started using a lot of drugs. One night when he was really high, a guy from his neighborhood talked him into going along on an armed robbery. This time when he got caught, instead of going back to a detention center where he had already spent a lot of time, he was sentenced to an adult prison. Many of the men there were doing hard time for big crimes. Even with all that he'd been through before, John was never so scared.

A kind older man in the next cell took John under his wing. He gave John a lot of good advice and told him what he needed to do to survive in prison. After getting to know John for about a month he invited him to go to a prayer group. He told John that it wasn't a strictly religious type group. He said the men prayed together and talked about ways they could live each day so their lives had purpose even though a lot of them were never going to get out.

At first John wasn't sure about going. He said he thought it was going to be a lot of talk about sinning and going to Hell. But after going to a few meetings, he found that he really liked it. He liked being around those guys. He felt more relaxed, safer—even at peace when he was around them.

The things they said made John see that he had to make some choices about the kind of life he wanted to lead. Once when we visited him, John said, "I felt like I woke up from a big sleep. I learned so much from those guys. Before going to this group, I never really thought about my spirituality—didn't really know what it meant."

The guys in the group explained spirituality in a way that made some sense to John. It explains how we feel too. The main points they made were:

1. There is a Higher Power—a loving, powerful force that is always there. This is the ultimate power source. Some people call this Higher Power God, Jesus, Allah—or whatever name expresses your connection to something bigger, something deeper than the material world around you. We're talking about a faith in something bigger than our own small selves.

2. Certain qualities will make your life work better. If you chose to use these spiritual qualities, you become a more genuinely powerful person. The main ones are—Honesty, Kindness, Patience, Generosity, Faith, Forgiveness, Courage to Do the Right Thing, and Love.

John started to realize that your highest authority isn't the judge, your parent, or probation officer—even though you have to answer to them, too. Your main authority is God or your Higher Power. That's who you really answer to. You can scam people. But you can't scam God. You can get away from the judge or your associates. But

226

you can't get away from God. God will love you no matter what. But God wants you to do the right thing. When you see the power in the spiritual qualities (mentioned before), you see that everything else is a fool's game.

Finding a Life Raft

Over the year, the way John saw the world changed in big ways. And the way he *felt* about things changed, too. By becoming open to a Higher Power, he stopped feeling so alone and hopeless. He saw that he was actually *never alone*—even when he was locked away from his family and friends, alone in his cell. John's faith in the fact that he was connected to a Higher Power gave him a feeling of safety and love. His faith gave him a strength he never felt before. He didn't have faith every minute. There were still times when he had his doubts and felt lost and scared. But from that time on, whenever he started feeling lost, before long he remembered his faith and connection. It was like his life raft. His faith and connection kept him going through the hardest and darkest times.

At times I felt like I grew up with a tombstone already over my head. But my spirituality makes me feel like I haven't been put on this earth just to live and die. It makes me feel like there is meaning and purpose for me in all this shit. My connection with God comforts and soothes me and gives me a sense of *well-being even when things in my life aren't going so well.*

Chrissy, 17 years old

Finding Your Connection?

A feeling of spiritual connection can come from lots of different sources. You don't have to belong to a group like John did to find it. Some people connect to their spiritual nature through religious programs or services and through reading their holy book like the Bible or Koran. Some people connect to their spirituality through rituals. Some people connect to their spiritual nature through a deep stillness and silence they find in meditation. Some people connect to their spiritual nature when they get out of their self-centered thoughts and experience the beauty around them—in nature, animals, and people.

How Do I Know There Is a Higher Power?

If you are waiting to get a signal out of the sky to prove that a Higher Power exists (like a bolt of lightning), you block yourself from the peace and relief that faith offers.

One young man summed up a common question that teens and young adults often have when he said, "If there is such a thing as God, then why do all of these shitty and horrible things happen to innocent people?" Many kids look at their lives and feel like they got "punished by God" for no reason. You have every right to feel angry if you were the victim of violence or emotional abuse. And

228

sometimes it feels easier to be angry at God for letting bad things happen to us than to be angry at the people who hurt us. There are no simple reasons for why painful things happen. But the truth is, no matter what, God does not want you to suffer.

So Where **Is** Your Faith?

Where you put your energy shows where your faith lies. Like John before he went to prison, maybe you think of yourself as a person who doesn't really have faith in anything. But that's not possible. *We are all people of faith.* You might put your energy or faith in the promises of street life or in connecting with a Higher Power. You might put your faith in violence or peace. You put your faith in fear and anger or love and forgiveness. A while ago on the subway, one of us saw a young man with the words "Thug Life" tattooed on his arm. In those two words he told the world where his faith was. But *genuine spiritual faith is something that lifts you up without bringing anyone else down.*

Only a spiritual path holds the potential for a comfort, peace, and safety that cannot be taken away. There might be times when you lose your connection, but it is there. There may be moments when fear or pain tempt you to put your faith in the "thug life." Remember, it's a false fix. Fears and negative thoughts may pull on you, but you can choose not to get caught up in them. Remind yourself of the deeper power found in a spiritual path—a faith with no strings attached.

Building Spiritual Muscle

These simple things can help make your faith or feeling of spirituality even more powerful.

Prayer

Everyone prays in their own language, and there is no language that God does not understand. —*Duke Ellington*

Asking

Help comes when we sincerely ask. It takes a lot of courage to ask—really ask—for help. Of course you can ask for anything you want in prayer. You can ask to get out of trouble. You can ask to have someone help you. You can ask to get a judge who sends you home. But next time you ask for something in prayer, remember to ask for help in what's going on in your inner world, too. Ask for help to know what is right and to do what is right. Ask for help to be patient. Ask how to make the most out of where you are. Admit that, by yourself, you might not know what the best thing to do is. Ask for guidance. Ask to see behind the masks that people wear to see the good in others. Ask for help to heal because God has the power to heal what we cannot heal alone. And the more you turn to God or a Higher Power, the lighter your load becomes.

Talking with Your Higher Power

Take time to have a real conversation with your Higher Power. Open your heart and listen. Maybe you've done things that you're ashamed of. Many people think if anyone really knew their darkest secrets, they'd be disgusted. But God can see the most hurtful things we've done and still love us completely. Although it might feel weird at first, know that this inner work is as important as anything that goes on around you.

Giving Thanks

With all of the losses you may have experienced and the pain you might feel, the idea of using prayer to give thanks might seem like a bad joke at first. Maybe it's hard to think of things to be grateful for. Giving thanks for the things you do have is a powerful form of prayer. When we begin to see what we are thankful for in our lives, we find that we have more and more to be grateful about. If you can find even one small thing to appreciate in life, it can make you feel more positive and hopeful. You can feel grateful even for small things like hot showers, food, and good music. *Remember the small things.* They're around you every day.

Stop and Think: What do you have to be grateful for right now? Offer thanks.

Being Still

While you are busy with your daily life, doing the things you do, there is a part of us that stays still. No matter what you are going through, it remains at peace. Getting in touch with this stillness puts you in touch with your spiritual nature. Meditation is a great way to tune into this peace.

The Big Job

Sometimes we think that little things don't matter. You might say, "So what if I pocket this money lying on the table?" "It's no big deal if I take the last seat on the bus while that old lady stands." "Yeah I punched my brother, but he'll get over it." But little things do matter. It all matters. The biggest part of flexing your spiritual muscle is understanding that even the smallest of our actions count.

We are all here on earth to perform the same job. The job that we all have is to work toward becoming more caring and responsible people. As you go through life you will have other jobs like going to school, making money, and taking care of your children. But the most important job anyone has is to shine a light of love, respect, and kindness into the world.

Chapter 16

The Future—What's in It for You?

I want my future to be healthy, wealthy, and have lots of happiness. I want to watch the sunrise every morning with the one I love. I want to see more opportunity for the next generation. I want my children to be more skilled and more educated so they can have a better life. But first I just want to get a good job.

Alex, 18 years old

Becoming Our Own Person

No matter how painful or difficult your past was, *this is your chance to decide who you want to be and how you will live.* You don't have to repeat the mistakes and bad decisions of your family. **Right now, you are free to build any kind of life you want.**

Being a kid means we are dependent on our family to take care of us. If they can't love us and give us what we need, we suffer. But as adults, we can take care of ourselves. We can be independent. We are free to become our own person. But if we get stuck in the pain of our past, it is hard to act upon our potential and promise. We let the present slip into the past. We lose time.

One Step at a Time

So what kind of future will you create? You may look around you and see adults in your life or in your community who are not living the kind of life that you want to have. Maybe they are struggling just to put food on the table. Some may have gone to jail or had problems with drugs and alcohol. They may be angry all of the time. They may have lost touch with their spiritual nature. You might look at these people and wonder if your path will be any different.

We've all felt nervous or worried about the future. It's natural. The thought of getting a job, maybe going to college, renting an apartment, and paying the bills can make us sweat. But don't get too stressed. Take a few deep breaths. Remind yourself of your strength, wisdom, and resilience. Take one step at a time.

How Long Will You Live?

Before you read this chapter about the future, answer this question as honestly as you can. How long do you think you'll live? Be as truthful as possible. Can you see yourself at 25 years old? How about at 40? Can you picture yourself as an old man or old woman? The answer to this question is key. If you don't see yourself as living past the age of 22, you might be thinking to yourself, "I might as well live large and go out with a bang." If this thought is sitting at the back of your mind, it will be very hard to convince yourself that you're worth the effort to heal. It will be tough to make the effort to live respectfully and with dignity.

Is Your Life a Stolen Car?

Think of it this way. If you steal a car, you would drive it fast and hard, right? You wouldn't care if it got dented, overheated, or if the seats got ripped. You are not invested in it. Easy come, easy go. But let's say you really wanted a car so you got a job and saved your money. You worked like a dog day in and day out. You passed up new clothes and stopped going to the movies so that you could save every penny for this car. Then comes the day when you finally drive it home. It is so beautiful, you can't believe it. You take pride in the effort that went into getting it. Are you going to smash it into a telephone pole on purpose? Are you going to let your drunk friend drive it to the store to get beer? No way. You have made a huge investment in this car. You want to have it for a long time.

It's the same deal with your life. If you don't see

yourself as living for more than a couple more years because of your high-risk lifestyle, you will probably have a "who gives a shit" attitude. You will end up driving your life like a stolen car. You will disrespect the rules of the road and of your spirit. You will be out of control and always on the run. If you want to have a life that lasts for more than a few more years, you have a much better chance if you *value* it.

Life on the Edge: Penthouse or Prison

Although you might not spend a lot of time actively thinking about your future, you probably have a lot of beliefs about what it'll be like. Lots of kids I talk to see themselves as either living the lifestyle of a professional basketball player or a professional prisoner (someone who is in and out of prison on a regular basis). They see their lives as either very rich or very poor. Very famous or the bottom of society. Many kids who engage in high-risk behaviors see themselves as living one of these extremes. It is easy to see why you would want to be a professional basketball player, actress, or famous musician. It looks like the good life. Plenty of money and lots of attention. In our minds we think these people get treated the way we all want to be treated—with dignity, power, and respect.

What is going on for the kids who see themselves having a career of imprisonment? Is it because by going to prison you don't run the risk of failing at school or a job? Is it because that is just what men or women in your family do? Does prison reflect the way you value yourself?

Doing Time: A Life on Hold

The first time I was arrested and sent to a detention center I was 13 years old. You see, I wanted to be arrested. I didn't have any family and I was lookin' for something— somewhere to belong. After being in the detention center, the staff and the other locked up kids became my family. I didn't want to leave when my time came. Where was I gonna go—to another foster family? I would even do self-destructive shit in order to stay. When I finally did leave, I knew I'd be back and I couldn't wait. As far as what I thought about my future, I believed what everyone always told me: I'd be dead or in prison before I was 18 years old. I thought I was nothin'. I thought I was shit. I could never sleep at night. So I stayed up late doin' push-ups and sit-ups making myself as strong as I could be. I figured since I was on my way to prison, then I'd be the baddest m********** there was. And actually I loved the idea of it. At least I started to feel like I knew who I was and what my future was. Lookin' back, I wish I had enough self-esteem and self-love to keep myself out of this hell hole rather than diving right in.

George, adult prisoner

While some kids put off taking the step into adulthood by remaining at home, others do it by making sure that they will never have to support themselves by going to prison. This may sound crazy at first. You might ask yourself, "Who would want to be locked up?" If you ask most people in prison, they will tell you that they would much rather be in their own homes surrounded by friends and family. But some people who are incarcerated feel more protected in prison than on the streets. In a way, it has become a lifestyle that they are used to. For one thing, they know the routine, they understand what is expected of them, and you can't flunk out.

In the outside world, becoming an adult means taking risks and challenges and possibly failing at them. If you honestly try to get a straight job, but are not successful, this might send you the message that you have failed. If you are in prison, very little is expected of you. Although you are stripped of your freedom, a lot of the pressure is taken off.

Tookie's Story

When Stanley "Tookie" Williams was seventeen-years-old he teamed up with Raymond Lee Washington to start the Crips. In April of 1981, Tookie was found guilty of murdering four people and was sent to San Quentin's death row. Over the years, Tookie grew to regret the violence that he and his gang caused. He does as much as he can from prison to guide young men and women away from tough street lives and prison. Tookie wrote a book called *Life in Prison* describing just what it's like to live your life locked up.[5] He writes about the humiliation, boredom, loss of freedom, and loneliness he has experienced. But when Tookie was young, he thought it would be cool to go to jail. He wanted to prove to the world how hard he was. Back then they called prison "gladiator schools." Now he sees how messed up his thinking was. He will never live on the outside again.

The term "prisoner" might not be a positive identity, but for many people it becomes one that they accept and understand. And as you work toward figuring out who you are and what you want do with your life, ask yourself if this is the identity that you want.

Remember, **the future does not arrive all at once**. It unfolds in front of us and is shaped by every small choice we make. At every moment, you have the power to shape your present and your future. If you see yourSelf as worthy, lovable, and good, you will make choices that honor a spiritual lifestyle. Each time the thought creeps in that you are no good, ruined, or a failure, take a deep breath and let those thoughts go. Watch them float away with no trace left to your mind. Remind yourSelf that at your core there is a bright, strong light.

Life in the Middle

What if there were another way to live your life? Let's call it a **Life in the Middle**. This life doesn't leave you in prison or in the penthouse. But it can be filled with all the joy and peace that the world offers. It might not be a financially rich life, but it can definitely be an emotionally and spiritually rich one. It might not have the glamour of a sport star's life, but it can give you the dignity of a life well lived. We think of a *life well lived* or a life in the middle as another lifestyle choice. It means living your life with respect, trust, love, and integrity. It means you make the right choices and get your power from the inside, not from what other people think of you. Living in the middle is not about the show, false power, hype, money, or fame. It's the satisfaction you get from doing life right.

Integrity—Its Own Reward

> Yeah, I'm a convicted felon, but I take a lot of pride in the fact that I have become a truly straight-up person. I spent a long time scamming to get what I wanted, but I got tired of the bitter taste it left in my mouth. When you are straight up and honest, it doesn't really matter if things go down the way you want them to. Because no matter what, you have your dignity. And being stand up is all about my honor. Honor is something that no one can take from you. It's what makes you a man.
>
> James, adult prisoner

Ever stood up to peer pressure because you knew that your friends were trying to get you hooked up in something that was just plain wrong? Well, *that's **integrity***.

Have you ever done the right thing—like returned money that someone lost even though you really needed cash? **That's integrity.** Have you ever told the truth even if it made you look uncool or embarrassed you? **That's integrity.** Integrity is **backbone**. It's having the courage to do what is right even if doesn't benefit you right then.

Sometimes when you show integrity, you even have to pay a price for your beliefs. But integrity is its own reward. It makes you stronger. It makes your life richer and more meaningful. It is your core Self showing through. People who use their integrity shine with a kind of power. They know that no matter what kind of mess swirls around them, their hearts will stay clean.

The Ins and Outs of a Life in the Middle

Now—let's get down to the nuts and bolts of a life in the middle. What kinds of benefits can you get from being a person who has a fairly typical job (like a bank teller, superintendent of a building, or a bus driver)? Let's say you have a family and a home. What kinds of gifts can a life like this give you? How would it feel to watch your children grow? How would it feel to come home to an apartment that you rent and see the furniture that you bought? How would it feel to kiss your partner in the evening? How would it feel to know that you don't have to look over your shoulder? You don't have to be nervous when a cop walks by. How would it feel to respect yourself because of the choices you made? How would it feel to have freedom because you are not in jail?

✋ **Stop and Think:** Take a minute and think of where you will be in five years. Where are you living? In the same neighborhood or have you moved on? What kind of job do you have? Are you married? Have any kids? What do you do with your free time (when you're not working)? Are you peaceful or angry?

Work—Everybody's Got to Do It

One of the most important and necessary parts of becoming independent is your ability to be productive and earn a living. This usually means getting and keeping a job. People find careers or jobs by taking a million different paths. Maybe you finish high school, go to college, and become a teacher. Or you could learn a trade and be an electrician, a plumber, or a carpenter. Maybe you start at a low-level job like a dishwasher and work your way up to a waiter, chef, or bartender. No matter what path you take, at some point in your life you will need to work.

✋ **Stop and Think:** What are your thoughts on working? These values often come from the people we grow up with. Think about your family for a minute. Do your parents work? Do they like their jobs or put up with jobs they hate in order to provide for their family? Do they work at all? What messages did they give you about the importance and value of working?

Am I My Job?

When I get out of here, I'm gonna snatch up

that McDonald's job. I'm gonna have that nasty grease on my hands, in my hair, and in my clothes. I'm gonna be rolling in that shit, because I am never comin' back to this joint.

(Michael talking about how he never wanted to be arrested for selling drugs and placed in a residential treatment center again.)

Michael, 16 years old

We think you can answer a lot of questions about how you see yourself as a worker by answering the question, "If you couldn't find any other legal job, would you work at McDonald's or would you do something illegal to make money instead?" I have spoken to many kids who would refuse to work at McDonald's or Burger King. They think that these kind of jobs are for losers. They would rather be selling drugs, getting busted, and going to jail. Somehow they don't see drug dealing as lowering themselves, but working at McDonald's is beneath them.

Although you might not want to work at McDonald's for the rest of your life, there is nothing shameful about *any* kind of honest work. But, for many kids, a job like working in McDonald's triggers their feelings of shame. Standing around in a McDonald's hat, having your friends come in and see you, feeling uncool, and not making a ton of money makes them feel vulnerable or weak. But in this job you are victimizing no one. You are not stealing. You are not increasing crime in a neighborhood. You are not trading away your freedom by going to jail. You are not feeding users' habits. You are not using your body in a violent or harmful way. You are making money honestly. You are dignified.

The Value of Work

Besides giving you a paycheck, what does work offer you? Here's a list that some kids came up with.

Become self-sufficient

More independent

Don't have to rely on other people to
get you the things you want

Accomplish something

Feel pride about something you did

Feel like you're making
something of yourself

Keeps you out of trouble

Make friends

Make your parents proud

It's your money so you
can do what you want with it

Self-esteem

Skills for future jobs

Working hard also gives us a sense of integrity. We know deep in our bones that we are on a good path. We have harmed no one. Perhaps we have even helped someone. In a way, working honestly and hard is like putting money in our spiritual piggy bank. It adds to who we are as people. It strengthens us.

Easy Money

At some point you might have found yourself drawn to the idea of **easy money**. It means making a lot of money by doing very little. Sometimes easy money is illegal and sometimes it's not. Think about how many people in your family or in your neighborhood buy lottery tickets. There's nothing wrong or illegal about buying tickets. It can even be fun. You get to dream a little about "what if I won." But we all know that very few people win. The chance of winning is one in a million.

There are other types of **easy money** which aren't "easy" at all. These are high-risk schemes that can take more away from us than the price of a lottery ticket. These are the types of illegal activities that promise to make us rich with no sweat. Lots of kids are serving sentences on drug- or weapon-related charges because they believed hustling drugs or selling guns would be easy money. Many thought, "I can make my own hours, no one is going to be watching over me all day telling me to do this or that, and I don't have to stand around in a store all day bored out of my mind." They sometimes even fool themselves into thinking that they'll be their own boss. Soon enough they learn that anyone hustling drugs is never their own boss. There is always someone watching what you do with their product. And if you screw up, you probably won't just get fired. The thing that these guys started to understand was that easy money isn't easy at all.

Just like some people think that working at Burger King makes you a chump, they think that making easy money makes you hard, tough, or big. The fantasy of easy money usually has more to do with the lifestyle than with the actual money that you might make. Maybe you have seen drug dealers driving a Mercedes or pulling out big wads of cash. And you want these things. Maybe you have seen people fear them. And you want this kind of false power. In reality, most drug dealers are dead or in jail by the time they are 30. But you already know this. The fantasy of easy money is very, very powerful. And every drug dealer has been pulled into penthouse or prison thinking. The problem is this: If you got your penthouse by selling drugs, you aren't going to be staying there long. You will not have the real respect, dignity, and power that living in the middle will give you. The easy money lifestyle requires you to constantly be snaking, lying, cheating, manipulating, power tripping, and selling yourself out. It blocks you from your spiritual Self and hands your power over to your supplier, the cops, and any thug who is out to take your trade.

Dealing with the Bumps in the Road

The future doesn't just happen to us. We make the future happen one step at a time. Sure, events happen to us. Sometimes they are good, sometimes they're not. **The future isn't about what happens to us as much as how**

we *deal* and *cope* with what happens to us. Let's say you lose your job because business is slow. You can get pissed off and say, "Why me?" You can sit around and blame the boss or you can take all that energy and put it into finding a new job. You can chose to see yourself as a victim or as a strong, resilient person who has a lot to bring to another job. We will all experience hardships and setbacks. What determines the quality of your future is how you chose to deal with them.

Every time you experience a challenging or difficult experience remind yourself that this one event is not all of who you are. It is not your entire present nor is it your entire future. *Don't forget to pick up your head and see the bigger picture.*

We Make Mistakes

Let's say that you read this book and it makes sense to you. Maybe you work on some of the issues facing you and really start to feel more control over your life. You realize that your family's problems do not have to define your life. You become more aware of your feelings and start to think more carefully about the choices that you make. Caring for others might come more easily to you. Anger will become something that you control, not something that controls you. Be realistic—no matter how much you grow and mature, you will always make mistakes. Making mistakes is part of being human.

We all find ourselves acting in ways that are not the best of who we are. At times we get disconnected from the Self. Mistakes can cause shame or leave us feeling like we just can't stay on track. We might get frustrated. If this

247

happens, be gentle with yourself. Don't throw in the towel. Don't get sucked in to using your mistakes as proof that you can't change or that it's too late for you to make something positive of your life. See the mistake for what it really is—one bad choice. Take responsibility, use the tools in this book to understand what triggered you, make things right if you can, ask for forgiveness, and move on.

Remember:

No mistake—no matter how big it seems—
can ever destroy the goodness of the Self.

I Meant It When I Said It

Many kids in jail or locked detention facilities do a lot of deep thinking. Sometimes being away from their friends and families gets them to think about their actions in a spiritual way. Their lives take on a bigger meaning than they felt it had on the streets. Many kids make promises to themselves about changing their attitudes or behavior. In a way, it's like they have seen a light turn on inside themselves. They see the world in a new way. They make big promises to themselves and to others about staying straight—and at the time they really, truly mean it.

But when they get back on the streets, reality hits. Old friends, old problems, and old ways of coping sometimes come back into play overnight. At this point it is easy to blow off the positive and hopeful thoughts you had when you were in detention. You might say, "Man, that wasn't really me. I was just thinking or feeling that because of where I was." You might tell yourself that lockup was not real life. Or it just might be hard to live up to the goals that you made for yourself when you were away from your neighborhood. And if you think you're going back to the streets and your neighborhood as a saint who never makes mistakes, you're expecting the impossible. We all make mistakes. If you expect yourself to be perfect, you are setting yourself up for failure. **It's not all or nothing.**

If you have read this book, the one thing we hope you got out of it is a chance to feel the power and dignity of yourSelf, even if it was for a few minutes here and there. **At least you know that there is a place of calm, wisdom, strength, and compassion inside of you.** No matter what choices you make in the future, Self is always with you, guiding you if you allow yourself to listen. Each crisis you face is an opportunity. It is an opportunity for you to hear the wise and loving voice you possess. In your life you will be asked to choose time and time again. Choose right from wrong, choose the loving path or the fearful one. Choose to give or to take. Choose to heal or to suffer. The louder you allow the voice of Self to become, the easier these choices become. You will become more confident in your ability to find the right path for you.

Stop and Think: Take a minute to think about the good things that you have in your life right now. Even if there is very little, try and find one good thing. Maybe it is your love of music or an aunt who makes you feel good about yourself. Now think of the things that you would like to have come to you in the future. Try and stay away from penthouse or prison thinking.

Think about the simple things in life that everyone can have. Think about a good meal at the end of the day. A job that you enjoy and that gives you satisfaction. Maybe you have a partner you love and who loves you. Maybe it is a chance to go on vacation to somewhere that you have always wanted to visit. Write down or say all of the things that you want to include in your future. Visualize these things coming to you from hard work and honesty. Open your heart and mind to the idea that you deserve these good things. Open your heart and mind to the idea that you are worthy of a good, safe, respectful life.

The Gift of Hope

Hope allows us to see the possibilities that are lying quietly in our Selves and our futures. Without hope, the future seems dark and frightening. But with hope, we give ourselves permission to reach out for the good things in life—like trust and love. No matter how bad things have been in the past, even one small grain of hope can carry us into our future. This might sound great, but what if you still don't feel so hopeful about your future? What if you look at your life, your family, and your friends and think the future will be as difficult and hurtful as the past? If this is the case, you need to actually **give yourself the gift of hope**.

How do you do that? Give yourself permission to believe that the future holds something worth living for. If you have a child, there is hope in the idea of raising your son or daughter with happiness and love. What do you want for your child? More than you had? If you said "yes" to this last question, then you have hope. If you have a passion or an interest, there is hope in the idea of following that dream through. If you love the idea of family, but have only experienced pain and rejection, there is hope in the thought that you will find a person to love and who will love you back. If you ever dreamed of accomplishing something like going to college, there is great hope in the idea of making this happen. **Give yourself permission to be hopeful about the future and you allow yourself to truly live.**

Only you can make your unique contribution to the world. Think about it. Nobody sees the world as you do. If you don't embrace hope and unleash the power of your love, your creativity, your sense of humor, and your spirit, no one can do it for you. You cannot be replaced. The world needs your voice, your opinion, and your wisdom. You are the power source. The world needs you to help it heal. Each time you make a choice that is honest, respectful, forgiving, and loving, you are actually healing the world. Whether you think about it like that or not, you are. And each time you make a choice that honors yourSelf, you become a larger, greater, deeper Being. This is the power of hope, and ultimately, the power of you.

Remind yourself often:

No matter what—the goodness of mySelf is right where I am.

The List
Hotlines for Help

There are people at these hotlines who can help you with a lot of different problems (for example, abuse, depression, suicidal thoughts). They will work with you to find the help you need.

Girls and Boys Town
1-800-448-3000
www.girlsandboystown.org

KidsPeace National Centers for Kids in Crisis
1-800-25 PEACE (or)
1-800-257-3223
www.kidspeace.org

Child Abuse

Childhelp USA
National Child Abuse Hotline
1-800-4-A-CHILD   (1-800-422-4453)
www.childhelpusa.org

Domestic Violence

National Domestic Violence Hotline
1-800-799-SAFE (1-800-799-7233)
1-800-787-3224 for TTY
www.thehotline.org

Pregnancy

Planned Parenthood Federation of America
1-800-230-PLAN (1-800-230-7526)
www.plannedparenthood.org

Growing Up Healthy Hotline
(For New York state only)
1-800-522-5006

Runaway

Both of these organizations can help you with many different crisis situations, not just running away from home.

Covenant House
1-800-999-9999
www.covenanthouse.org

National Runaway Switchboard
1-800-621-4000
www.nrscrisisline.org

Prostitution

Children of the Night
1-800-551-1300
www.childrenofthenight.org

Substance Abuse

Al-Anon/Alateen
1-888-4AL-ANON (1-888-425-2666)
www.al-anon.org
Both of these organizations are for people who have a relative or friends with an alcohol problem.

Families Anonymous
1-800-736-9805 (USA only)
1-847-294-5877 (outside USA)
www.familiesanonymous.org

National Council on Alcoholism and
Drug Dependence
1-800-622-2255
www.ncadd.org

Center for Substance Abuse Treatment (CSAT)
Drug Abuse Information and Treatment Referral Hotline
1-800-662-HELP (1-800-662-4357)
www.samhsa.gov

References

[1]Thanks to Joe Moore for his ideas about entitlement in his manual *Search Out Another Road (S.O.A.R)*: *A Short Course of Reflection on Life Choices and Life Changes*.

[2]Elisabeth Kübler-Ross. *On Death and Dying*. New York: Macmillan, 1969.

[3]*Homeboys: Life and Death in the Hood*. Director Donna Dewey/Active Parenting/www.activeparenting.com

[4]Azim Khamisa. *Azim's Bardo: A Father's Journey from Murder to Forgiveness*. Los Altos, CA: Rising Star Press, 1998.

[5]Stan Tookie Williams. New York: Morrow, 1998.

Tell Us What You Think?

If Power Source helped you or made a difference in your life we'd love to hear about it.

You can write to us at:

The Lionheart Foundation
Box 170115
Boston, MA 02117

NOTES

NOTES

Ordering Information

Power Source can be ordered through the Lionheart Foundation. After the Lionheart Foundation reaches its goal of free distribution to every major program for youth-at-risk in the United States, if Lionheart has funds to print additional books, free copies will be sent to youth and young adults (upon request) who do not have the means to pay.

Individual copies: $15 (includes shipping)

Bulk rates are available for orders of over nine copies.

For orders outside of the U.S. and Canada, please send only checks drawn on a U.S. bank in U.S. dollars, or an international postal money order in U.S. dollars.

We accept Visa, Mastercard, or check or money order payable to:

The Lionheart Foundation
Box 170115
Boston, MA 02117

For counselors, clergy, and volunteers: The *Power Source* Facilitator's Manual with guidance and suggestions for facilitating groups based on *Power Source* can be ordered through the Lionheart Foundation. See **www.lionheart.org**